KNOW YOUR
HOBBY ANIMALS

A BREED ENCYCLOPEDIA

172 Breed Profiles of Chickens, Cows, Goats, Pigs, and Sheep

JACK BYARD

Fox Chapel
PUBLISHING
www.FoxChapelPublishing.com

T0051184

Originally published by Old Pond Publishing Ltd under the titles *Know Your Sheep*, *Know Your Cows*, *Know Your Pigs*, *Know Your Chickens*, and *Know Your Goats*. Copyright © Jack Byard, 2019, 2020

Fox Chapel Publishers International Ltd. All rights reserved.

This edition copyright © 2020 by Fox Chapel Publishing Company, Inc.,
903 Square Street, Mount Joy, PA 17552. All rights reserved. Published under license.

ISBN 978-1-4971-0087-9

Library of Congress Control Number:2019957175

To learn more about the other great books from Fox Chapel Publishing, or to find a retailer near you, call toll-free 800-457-9112 or visit us at *www.FoxChapelPublishing.com*.

We are always looking for talented authors. To submit an idea, please send a brief inquiry to acquisitions@foxchapelpublishing.com.

Printed in Singapore
First printing

NOTE: All weights, sizes, and measurements in this book are averages based on breed records and the terrain in which the animals live.

This book has been published with the intent to provide accurate and authoritative information in regard to the subject matter within. While every precaution has been taken in the preparation of this book, the author and publisher expressly disclaim any responsibility for any errors, omissions, or adverse effects arising from the use or application of the information contained herein.

CONTENTS

FOREWORD

Sheep, goats, pigs, cows, and chickens have provided us with food and drink, clothing, and shelter for thousands of years. Today many breeds are extremely rare and not commercially viable, and this is where the smallholder—the hobby farmer—plays a crucial role. After a full day at the office, workshop, or local store, they will put in several hours looking after their charges. Some keep a donkey or mule in the field with the sheep, natural guardians against attack from four-legged predators, such as foxes, coyotes, and bobcats (and against being stolen by the two-legged variety on occasion).

In most countries of the world, there are areas that are inaccessible to agricultural machinery. What keeps the moors and hills surrounding my home so neat and trim, making it accessible to lovers of the open countryside? It is the hill sheep that roam this unfenced and harsh land. Certain breeds of draft horse are increasingly used for forestry work in areas out of bounds to machinery, being more efficient and less damaging to the landscape.

Organizations such as The Livestock Conservancy in the United States and the Rare Breeds Survival Trust in the UK work tirelessly to protect these rare breeds, but more needs to be done. We must never forget the value of these animals—they have supported us for generations, after all—and protect farmers and ranchers, both large and small, from those who profess to know better.

—Jack Byard, Bradford, England, 2020

CHICKENS

Our feathered friend and companion, the chicken, has been around "since Adam were a lad," as an old farming friend used to say.

The rich diversity of color, size, and feather pattern, along with their elegant toy-soldier-like strutting, is a joy to behold. Most are friendly, docile creatures but there are a few "grumpy old men" who will view your legs as their next appetizer. In the chicken world, many are bred for the sheer joy, pleasure, and happiness they give to their breeders. Many small breeders will put in two or three hours of care on top of a full day at work.

Standards of care for chickens vary enormously around of world, but thankfully the welfare of the birds is widely promoted, and most chicken farming is undertaken responsibly these days. The vast majority of British farms and farmers ensure that all birds have a good and stress-free life, and lead the way in commercial standards of husbandry, while in the United States bodies such as the Animal Welfare Institute promote high welfare standards and animal-sensitive approaches to farming.

In the British Isles, organizations such as The Rare Poultry Society and the Rare Breeds Survival Trust (RBST) do much to ensure that rare breeds do not disappear into the annals of history. RBST grading, where mentioned in the book, refers only to the color of the chicken pictured. The same breed, but of a different color, can have a different grade.

Note: Many breeds of chicken have been developed to produce a range of different varieties/colors. In this book, the breed heading and characteristics information relate to the variety shown in the accompanying photograph.

Ancona

Characteristics

Color: Midnight blue with bright V-shaped white speckles.

One of the oldest breeds of chickens, the Ancona was bred for centuries in the Marche region on the east coast of Italy. Fortunately, it was spotted by a group of poultry enthusiasts and arrived in the British Isles in the mid- to late-nineteenth century. It was also known as the Mottled Leghorn or Black Leghorn, since its beautiful patterned plumage gives it a strong resemblance to that breed. The feathers whiten with age.

This tough, hardy bird is extremely popular in Europe since it can adapt easily to a range of environments. It is an efficient scavenger and has a great instinct for finding food. It is also well known for its egg-laying abilities; it is quite common for one bird to lay 300 white eggs a year. As a result of this range of attributes, the breed has flourished. The high-flying Ancona must always be bred free range but kept within a high fence to prevent it from disappearing.

It is no longer used commercially but is bred for the pleasure it gives, still having a firm place in domestic flocks and at poultry shows throughout the British Isles, Europe, and the United States.

Andalusian

Characteristics

Color: Slate-blue with narrow, dark blue lacing on each feather.

This ornamental bird was developed in Andalusia, Spain, and further developed in the British Isles and the United States. The modern blue Andalusian is a result of crossing black and white birds imported from Andalusia in 1846. Crossing two blue birds will result in 25 percent black and 25 percent white, with the remaining 50 percent of the clutch blue. The Andalusian is therefore only bred by enthusiasts with an interest in preserving the breed. The development of the breed as we know it today is credited to the English, but whether this was achieved in Andalusia or in England is not known.

The Andalusian has a magnificent presence, being both elegant and graceful (the reasons most people give for keeping them). It is also an extremely fast runner (the breed society suggests anyone wishing to keep the birds should invest in a landing net). One bird will lay around 160 creamy white eggs a year.

Originally from Andalusia in Spain, the breed is now found throughout Europe, the British Isles, the United States, Canada, and Australia.

Appenzeller Spitzhauben

Characteristics

Silver Spangled

Color: Silvery white with a lacy bonnet; feather tips have black dots (spangles).

Also Gold Spangled, Black Spangled, and Barthuhner varieties.

The Appenzeller—the national chicken breed of Switzerland—originated in the Canton of Appenzeller, where it is thought to have existed for over 40 years. The bird's comb is similar to a traditional pointed lace bonnet from the area: a *spitzhauben*.

During World War II, the Appenzeller Spitzhauben came close to extinction, and it was only the dedication of German breeders in the 1950s that ensured its survival. It is a good, hardy breed, well adapted to living in mountainous regions. The birds require little attention if they have a good foraging area and virtually look after themselves. The Appenzeller does not like to be confined and is at its best when given the freedom to roam; the birds are superb climbers and will happily roost in trees. It will lay in the region of 150 eggs a year so is possibly not the best of layers, but is "a good companion."

Originally found only in Switzerland, the breed is now seen throughout the British Isles and Europe, the United States, Canada, and Australia.

Araucana

Characteristics

Lavender

Color: Blue-gray, with a small pea comb.

Also Blue, Black/Red, Silver Duckwing, Golden Duckwing, Blue/Red, Pile, Crele, Spangled, Cuckoo, Black and White varieties.

The Araucana is an ancient breed and was named after the Araucano tribe of Native South Americans who lived on the high plains of the Andes Mountains in Chile. In the early sixteenth century, the Portuguese explorer Magellan recorded seeing blue-egg-laying poultry resembling the Araucana, and later in the same century the breed arrived in countries around the Mediterranean. The British type of Araucana was developed in Scotland by George Malcolm from birds carried on a Chilean ship that was wrecked in the Hebrides in the 1930s.

The Araucana does not lay many eggs, but the eggs are spectacular: mainly blue or green but ranging from greenish-blue to violet-blue to grayish. The shell is unique in that it is the same color both inside and out. The Araucana are hardy, grow quickly, and mature fast. They are content to be housed in a pen as long as there is a regular supply of fresh grass.

It is believed that in 2006 the Spangled variety became extinct, but hopefully in some remote corner of the world there are still Spangled Araucana to be found. The breed originated in the Andes, but varieties are now found worldwide.

Australorp

Characteristics

Black

Color: Black with green sheen.

Also Blue and White varieties.

The Australorp was developed from the Black Orpington. William Cook's Orpingtons were imported into Australia from the British Isles in the nineteenth century. Australian breeders wanted a quality dual-purpose breed, and this was achieved by crossing the Black Orpington with the Langshan, Minorca, the White Leghorn, and a touch of Rhode Island Red. The Australorp was born. Several people wanted to take the credit for choosing the name "Australian Laying Orpington," but it didn't exactly trip off the tongue! In 1919, Arthur Harwood suggested "Austral" with an added "orp" to honor the bird's ancestors, and the name was accepted. In 1921, the breed was imported into the British Isles.

It is a beautiful bird and a good all-round breed, laying around 250 light brown eggs a year. A group of six Australorps hold the world record (1922–1923) for laying 1,857 eggs, an average of 309.5 eggs per hen, over 365 consecutive days. They make good pets, being docile and friendly, and are happy in a run or free range: a good choice for a beginner. From its origins in Australia, the breed is now found throughout the British Isles and most major continents.

Barnevelder

Characteristics

Double Laced

Color: Double-laced mahogany/black feathers; the male's have iridescent shades of green.

Also Black, Partridge and Silver varieties.

Developed during the nineteenth century in Barneveld, Holland, the breed was originally created to produce beautiful dark brown eggs. The breeds used were chosen with great care. A Dutch hen was crossed with a Langshan, producing dark-colored eggs; further crosses with the Buff Orpington, Brahma, and Cochin were introduced to improve the quality and color of the eggs. From 1910, steps were taken to introduce uniformity to the Barnevelder. In 1921, the Dutch Association of Barnevelder Breeders was formed and the breed standard fixed. In the same year, the breed was imported into the British Isles, and the British Barnevelder Club formed.

The breed became famous, leading to worldwide exports. This good, hardy, dual-purpose hen is capable of laying an average of 200 dark brown, good-flavored eggs each year. The Barnevelder is a lazy chicken and must be kept free range to ensure it receives plenty of exercise; overweight Barnevelder do not lay eggs. The chicks are born yellow, and the brown feathers develop as the bird matures.

From its origins in Holland the breed is now found worldwide.

Belgian d'Uccle

Characteristics

Mille Fleur

Color: Rich red/brown; in the middle of each feather is a black iridescent crescent band; each feather is tipped with a white "half moon."

Also Black, Blue, Lavender Quail, Silver Quail, Blue Quail, Cuckoo, Lavender Mottled, and Black Mottled varieties.

Developed in Uccle on the southeastern border of Belgium by Michel Van Gelder, a rich Dutch businessman in the late nineteenth century, the Mille Fleur ("a thousand flowers") was one of the first d'Uccle breeds. It is understood to be a cross of the Dutch Sabelpoot bantam and the Barbu d'Anvers bantam, but Michel was a frequent visitor to British and German poultry shows, so it is possible that breeds from these countries were used to "improve" the d'Uccle.

It is frequently confused with the Booted Bantam, but that only has boots, and the d'Uccle has a beard, muffs, and boots. When seen together, the difference is obvious. It is a docile, friendly, and talkative breed that will happily sit in your hand or on your shoulder.

Originally from Belgium, the breed is now found throughout the British Isles and Europe, Australia, and the United States.

Black Rock

Characteristics

Color: Beautiful blue/black plumage that glows in the sunshine, with a collar of gold-colored feathers extending down to the stomach. The gold patterning on front and neck differs on each bird.

The Black Rock is a hybrid, resulting from crossing a Rhode Island Red male with a Plymouth Rock female. The gold color comes from the Rhode Island Red, and the silver from the Plymouth Rock. The sex of the Black Rock can be determined at a day old, and as a result the male Black Rock is rarely seen. Peter and Margaret Siddons looked after and improved the breeding stock in Scotland for forty years; following their retirement, Eddie Lovett and his son Calum took on the task.

This attractive, hardy breed, with its thick plumage, is more than capable of coping with the vagaries of weather. Even though the chicks are vaccinated at a day old, the breed has a natural, highly developed immune system. This busy and inquisitive bird is easy to handle, but given half a chance would roost in a tree. An ideal pet for older children, it will lay up to 300 medium to dark brown eggs a year. The Black Rock enjoys freedom, and becomes bored if confined.

Originally from the United States, the breed is now found throughout the British Isles and on most major continents.

Brahma

Characteristics

Gold

Color: Head and neck rich gold; feathers have central black stripe; body dull red-black; tail shiny black. Back gold, underbody glossy black.

Also Dark, Light, White, Blue Partridge, and Buff Columbian varieties.

For many years the true origin of the Brahma—said to have been named after the Brahmaputra River in India—has been debated. Most breeders now agree that the breed developed in the United States from breeds imported from Shanghai, China, in the 1840s. A group of nine "Brahmas" arrived in the British Isles in the mid-nineteenth century as a gift for Queen Victoria, where their appearance caused quite a stir.

The dual-purpose Brahma will lay around 150 brown-tinted eggs a year. Today they are mainly bred for ornamental use. The feathered legs and feet must be kept clean and dry to avoid serious damage. Described as large, stately, docile, and trusting, they will roam happily in a garden with a low fence, and they make great pets.

Originally from the United States, the breed is now found throughout the British Isles and on most major continents.

Cochin

Characteristics

Buff

Color: Rich blending shades of cinnamon, gold, and lemon.

Also Black, Blue, Cuckoo, Partridge and Grouse, and White varieties.

The Cochin (or Chinese Shanghai Fowl as it was originally known) originated in China more than 150 years ago and was imported into the United States and the British Isles in the 1800s. The first arrivals in the British Isles—large, friendly "balls of fluff and feather"—were hugely popular when they were presented to Queen Victoria. The bird stood out from other breeds on account of the large number of feathers covering the feet and legs, and bore no resemblance to any known breed at the time; it became an overnight success and a "must-have" breed. In 1853, *Punch* magazine recorded one being sold for £2,587 (roughly £86,000 [or about $113,000] in today's currency) during what became known as the "Cochin Craze." More Cochin were imported to the British Isles, and the breed was improved and developed thereafter, continuing the work that had already been started in the United States.

The Cochin is cold hardy. In summer its thick feather coat can lead to overheating, but a gentle water spray will keep them cool, happy, and healthy. It lays around 150 to 180 brown eggs a year.

The Cochin originated in China and is now found throughout the British Isles and most major continents.

Croad Langshan

Characteristics

Black

Color: Black with beetle-green luster.

Also White and Blue varieties.

The Langshan was imported into the British Isles in 1872 by Major F. T. Croad. The "Croad" part of the name was added in tribute to Miss A. C. Croad, the major's niece, who gave unstinting support during the development and improvement of the Croad Langshan. It was developed from an ancient breed from the Langshan district of northern China, where the original breed can still be found. The Maran, Barnevelder, and Black Orpington were developed using the Croad Langshan. In the early 1900s, it was a popular dual-purpose breed—the breed club opening in 1904—and remained so until after World War II when, as with many other breeds, numbers went into serious decline. It was only the intervention of The Rare Poultry Society that prevented extinction.

This graceful, intelligent, inquisitive, and docile bird prefers dry, sheltered conditions and is adaptable from free range to small, open enclosures. The Croad Langshan lays up to 200 eggs a year. Eggs are brown with a plum-colored bloom.

Originating in Asia, the breed is now found throughout the British Isles, Europe, the United States, and Australia.

Dorking

Characteristics

Silver Gray

Color: Male black with silver white hackle and saddle. Hen gentle shades of slate-gray with black-striped hackle and salmon breast.

Also Red, Dark, Cuckoo, and White varieties.

Bred in Italy during the reign of Julius Caesar (100 to 44 BC), the Dorking is one of the oldest breeds of domesticated poultry. It also has five toes, four being more usual, which is a further indication of its ancient origins. "When you look at Dorkings, you are looking at history!" This superb dual-purpose breed was brought to the British Isles by the Romans, and it is here that most of the development and improvement has taken place. The Dorking has also been used to develop many of the modern breeds. It had its debut in 1845 at a British poultry show, many hundreds of years after its introduction.

The Dorking is one of the few breeds with red earlobes to lay white eggs (around 140 eggs a year). Fewer than 500 breeding pairs are known to exist. It is a large, docile bird, and to grow and remain healthy must have a large area in which to exercise and forage. It produces excellent meat and eggs.

The Dorking is found throughout the British Isles, Europe, the United States, and Australia.

Dutch Bantam

Characteristics

Gold Partridge

Color: Male hackle shaded dark to light orange; dark green central stripe on feathers. Breast black with green sheen; shoulders deep reddish-brown; wing bar iridescent green. Main tail feathers iridescent green-black.

Also Silver Partridge, Yellow Partridge, Blue Silver Partridge, plus at least another twelve varieties.

There is written evidence that the breed was introduced into Holland in the seventeenth century by the sailors of the Dutch East India Company who had collected the birds from the Bantam Islands in the Dutch East Indies. The name *bantam* has no connection with the island; it was common practice to call small fowl *bantams*. Old Dutch paintings show chickens similar to the Dutch Bantam, as do British paintings from the 1860s. Its early popularity can be explained by a law in existence at the time that stipulated that all large eggs must be given to the Lord of the Manor. The bantam, producing small eggs, removed the problem.

The birds are active and, if handled regularly, become very friendly. Because of their diminutive size, they are ideal for small spaces, but a good aviary or a high fence is a necessity as they are good flyers. The Dutch Bantam is a true bantam; it has no large fowl equivalent.

Originally only in the Netherlands, the breed is now found throughout the British Isles and worldwide.

Faverolles

Characteristics

Salmon

Color: Male iridescent black, bronze back, black wings, straw-colored hackle. Hen brown and creamy-white, as are beard and muffs.

Also Black, Blue Laced, Buff, Cuckoo, Ermine, and White varieties.

The breed comes from the village of Faverolles in northern France and was developed from a cross of the Houdan, Cochin and Dorking (this ancestry giving the Faverolles five toes). There are three different types of Faverolles: the original French, the German, and the British. The latter was imported into the British Isles in 1886 and consequently crossed with the Orpington, the Sussex, and the Indian Game to produce the dual-purpose breed we know today. A French writer once said, "As farmyard fowls they stand unrivalled, their superiority being uncontestable."

This genteel, sweet-natured bird, an ideal breed for children, has been described as the peacock or French poodle of the chicken world. Whatever its description, it certainly stands out in a crowd with its creamy white beard and muffs. It lays around 160 light brown or creamy eggs throughout the year.

The Faverolles originated in France but is now found in the British Isles, Europe, and most major continents.

Golden Phoenix

Characteristics

Color: Male head and neck amber, shading to golden buff at shoulder. Chest and wings green; downy white fluff on saddle. Tail black, glowing purple-green in sunlight.

This striking bird originated in Japan where it was known as the Onagadori, the long-tailed breed of chicken that had been bred there for 1,000 years and kept in the Imperial Gardens. The tail feathers of this exceptional bird could reach 27 feet (8.25 meters) in length. In the 1800s, the Onagadori was crossed with German game birds with the purpose of breeding out health problems. Further developments were carried out in the United States using the Leghorn, again with the intention of improving the health and well-being of the Golden Phoenix. This crossing had the effect of breeding out the gene responsible for the exceptional tail feathers, but a modern mature male can still have a tail up to 3 feet (1 meter) long.

The Golden Phoenix is well adapted to free range, but this can be at the cost of the tail feathers. A good roost well clear of the ground will give it the best of both worlds. They make good mothers, are docile but not too friendly, and have been known to chase off marauding cats taking too close an interest in their brood.

Originally from Japan, the breed is now found worldwide.

Hamburg

Characteristics

Silver Spangled

Color: Lustrous greenish-black spangles on silvery-white background, almost like polka dots. End of each feather has half-moon-shaped black spangle.

Also Black, Gold Penciled, Silver Penciled, and Gold Spangled varieties.

With a history dating back to the 1600s, it is not surprising that the Hamburg's country of origin—despite the name—is unclear. The Spangled variety was developed in Yorkshire and Lancashire in the 1700s. A small breed, but capable of laying a good quantity of medium-sized eggs (around 150 a year), it is inconceivable that the Hamburg has not been used to improve the egg-laying capabilities of other breeds, but there is no solid evidence for this. It was once known as the "Dutch Everyday Layer," but its use is now mainly ornamental. The Hamburg also goes by the name "Moonies and Crescent" because of its spangles.

Stylish, *elegant*, and *snappy* are adjectives often used to describe this beautiful bird. Its appearance will brighten even the darkest of days. The Hamburg thrives best when free range, is an efficient forager, and capable of flying a good distance.

Originally found in Holland and Germany, the Hamburg has spread to the British Isles, Europe, the United States, and Australia.

Indian Game

Characteristics

Dark

Color: Male glossy black with trace of deep chestnut in wings. Hen rich mahogany with glossy black double lacing around feathers.

Also Jubilee and Blue Laced varieties.

The Indian Game is a beautiful old British poultry breed. It was developed in Cornwall in southwest England in the early nineteenth century by Sir Walter Raleigh Gilbert, crossing the ancient fighting breeds of Red Asil, Malay, and Old English Game to produce fighting birds. It proved a failure, being too heavy as a fighter, and cockfighting was banned soon after in 1847. However, it was soon realized that the breed's true worth was in the quality of its excellent meat, a trait that is valued to this day. It has also been crossed with the Dorking and Sussex breeds with superb results. The breed was first shown at The Crystal Palace in Hyde Park, London, in 1858, but was rarely seen outside Cornwall until the end of the nineteenth century.

Although poor layers, producing about 80 light brown eggs per year, they are attentive mothers. Today this proud, elegant bird, in its purest form, is seen at poultry shows around the world.

Originally from Cornwall, the Indian Game is now seen throughout the British Isles and worldwide.

Japanese Bantam

Characteristics

Black Tailed White

Color: Pure white with black tail and red face, yellow legs.

Also Blue, Brown Red, Grey, Birchen, Silver, Dark, and Millers (thirty-five varieties in all).

The development of the Japanese Bantam or Chabo (a Japanese word for *dwarf*) goes back to at least the seventeenth century, at which time it could be seen waddling through the gardens of the rich and famous in Japan. A cross of breeds from China and South East Asia, it arrived in Europe in the 1700s and was a feature in Japanese and Dutch art during that period.

The Japanese Bantam has very short legs and, given its "U"-shaped profile and rounded shape, its appearance, when walking, is duck-like. It is a small, attractive bird with a large tail that can stand a third higher than its head. It is an ideal small garden chicken, small and light; because of its short legs it will do little harm to lawn or garden. This breed makes an ideal pet for children, being calm, docile, and friendly, and with good care will live for more than ten years. The Japanese is a true bantam; it has no larger fowl equivalent.

Originally only in Japan, the Japanese Bantam can now be found in the British Isles and on most major continents.

Jersey Giant

Characteristics

Black

Color: Shiny black with green sheen; underbody slate-gray.

Also White and Blue varieties.

The breed was developed by the brothers John and Thomas Black of Burlington County, New Jersey, United States, in the late nineteenth century, and accepted as a breed in 1922. It was developed from crosses of the Dark Brahma, Black Java, and Black Langshan, and possibly the Black Orpington. The breed is named after the brothers, not the color of the original Jersey Giant. The Black variety was followed in 1947 by the White, and it was not until almost forty years later that the Blue variety appeared. A superb dual-purpose breed, the original concept was to produce a large table bird as an alternative to the turkey; a mature Jersey Giant weighs in at an average of 13 lb (5.9 kg). It is the largest chicken breed in the world.

The Jersey Giant is cold hardy and, despite its size, calm and gentle. They are too slow growing for commercial breeders, but the quality is worth waiting for. The eggs are in keeping with the size of the bird: the hen lays around 160 large light to dark brown eggs a year.

Originally from the United States, the Jersey Giant is now found in the British Isles and on most major continents.

Lakenvelder

Characteristics

Color: Black head, neck, and hackle. Body mostly soft white feathers.

Also Blue Marked variety.

The Dutch believe the breed is named after the village of Lakenvelt in Holland and point out they have breeds of goats and cattle with black heads and tails called Lakenvelder (which translates as "shadow on a sheet"). The Germans argue that it may have a Dutch name but that it was developed in Westphalia, Germany. Records show the Lakenvelder was around in the early eighteenth century but did not flap a wing in the British Isles until the beginning of the twentieth century. With its striking black and white coloring, this breed certainly stands out in the crowd.

It is a fairly small bird, the male weighing about 5½ lb (2.5 kg), but is very active and adaptable. It will live contentedly in a confined area but is much happier free range. The bird lays an average of 160 white or creamy-white eggs per year. One breeder describes them as being "independently minded little souls, preferring to forage rather than eat the grain supplied and will roost in trees in all weathers."

Originally from the Netherlands, the breed is now found in the British Isles, Europe, and on most major continents.

Leghorn

Characteristics

Brown

Color: Head and hackle orange shading to pale yellow; back, shoulders, and wings deep red or maroon.

Also Black, Buff, Cuckoo, Blue, Golden Duckwing, Silver Duckwing, Exchequer (black and white checkered), Black Mottled, Red Mottled, Partridge, and White varieties.

The Leghorn is named after the Italian city of Livorno. It found its way to the United States in the 1830s and arrived in the British Isles at the latter end of the nineteenth century, and it was here that most of the colored breeds were developed. The Leghorn was crossed with the Malay and the Minorcan to improve the quality and size of the eggs. The Leghorn is well represented in the world of advertising: most cockerels depicted are slim, have large combs, and long curved tail feathers.

The Leghorn is one of the best-known breeds in the world, producing the majority of the global supply of white or pearly white eggs. A good white Leghorn will lay in the region of 300 eggs a year, the Black and Brown laying slightly less (up to 250 a year). It is a strutting, noisy bird, a bird with presence, a good forager, and capable of flying a good distance. If available, it will happily roost in a tree.

Originally from Italy, the Leghorn is now found worldwide.

Maran

Characteristics

Copper Headed Black

Color: Black with green sheen. Male has copper neck and saddle hackles; hen has rich copper-colored feathers head and neck.

Also Black, Dark Cuckoo, Golden Cuckoo, and Silver Cuckoo varieties.

When the Duke of Anjou, later to become Henry II, married Eleanor of Aquitaine in the twelfth century, part of her dowry was land in southwest France. Thereafter, British ships would call at La Rochelle, near Maran; they would exchange the survivors of onboard cockfights for fresh poultry, eggs, and fresh food. These survivors would breed with the local marsh hens, and it is thought that this is how the Maran began life. The breed as we know it today arrived in the British Isles in 1929 courtesy of Lord Greenway who brought eggs back from the Paris Exhibition and started to breed them selectively to standardize the color. Today there are five standard colors in the British Isles and twelve in France. The Copper Headed Maran, an attractive and popular member of the Maran family, was first shown in the 1930s.

The Maran is known for quality meat but most of all for laying up to 200 beautiful chocolate-brown eggs each year.

Originally from France, the Maran is now found in the British Isles, Europe, the United States, and Canada.

Marsh Daisy

Characteristics

Wheaten

Color: Male's hackles rich gold; back and wing bows deeper gold; body golden brown; tail beetle-green black.

Also Brown variety.

The Marsh Daisy was developed by John Wright in Marshside, Lancashire in northern England at the latter end of the nineteenth century; this work was continued by Charles Moor. The name has two possible origins: either the marshy area where it was developed, or the remarkable resemblance of its comb to the Marsh Daisy flower. A good range of poultry went into the melting pot to produce this magnificent breed: Black Hamburg, White Leghorn plus Malay and Old English Game, with Pit Game and Sicilian Buttercup being added by John Moor in 1913.

It is one of the rarest breeds even in the British Isles, where it is looked after by The Rare Poultry Society. It was at one time believed to be extinct until Ralph White found a flock in the Williton area of Somerset in 1971. This is a very gentle breed, including the male birds. It is particularly happy free range and not troubled by the rain; it is a good flyer and lays about 160 to 200 eggs a year. Originally there were five colors: Wheaten, Brown, Buff, Black, and White. The Buff, Black, and White are thought to be extinct.

Originally from Lancashire, there are today a few throughout the British Isles and the world.

Old English Game

Characteristics

Black Breasted Silver Duckwing (Oxford)

Color: White neck and saddle, breasts and thighs black; back, shoulders, and wings silver-white; wings have steel-blue bar; tail black.

Two categories: Carlisle (back horizontal to ground); Oxford (back 45° to ground).

The Old English Game has been strutting around the pens of the British Isles for more than 200 years, descended from the ancient fighting cock known as "Pit Game." During the Roman occupation, a breed similar to the Old English Game was recorded. It would appear that over the last 2,000 years its appearance and personality have changed very little, if at all.

Cockfighting in the British Isles became illegal in 1849, and the attractive Old English Game is now bred as a purely ornamental show bird. It is extremely aggressive, and not for the inexperienced breeder. Two males put together will fight to the death; the females can be equally aggressive and are very protective of their young. Despite being noisy and refusing to be confined, they are still one of the most popular game birds. Choose any of the almost sixty colors and you cannot fail to be exhilarated by their appearance and the assured presence of the male.

Originally found in the British Isles, the breed is now seen in Europe, the United States, Canada, and Australia.

Orpington

Characteristic

Buff

Color: Buff-colored feathers, red face, comb, and wattles; earlobes creamy-white.

Also Blue, Black and White, and Gold Laced varieties, and rarely seen Jubilee.

The Orpington was developed in a Kent village in southeastern England in the nineteenth century by William Cook, the son of a hostler who decided to work with chickens instead of horses. He became deeply involved in poultry as a journalist, advisor, and lecturer, and made his small village of Orpington world-famous. The first Orpingtons were black, very similar in appearance to the Langshan, and were bred in 1886 by crossing the Minorca, Langshan, and Plymouth Rock. There are many rich color variations for this extremely attractive bird: the original Black, the very popular Buff (developed in 1894 due to public demand), Blue, White, and Gold Laced.

This is a dual-purpose breed, laying in the region of 180 brown eggs a year. The Orpington is adaptable and can be kept in a small pen but free range is the better option. They have a tendency to overeat and need plenty of exercise. Docile, affectionate, and easily handled, they make ideal pets.

Originally found only in the British Isles, the breed is now seen in the United States, Canada, and Australia.

Pekin

Characteristics

Color: Male's head dark red, shading through orange or red-gold, lighter toward shoulders; underbody green-black. Back, shoulders, and wing bows crimson.

Also Cuckoo, Mottled, Barred, Birchen, Colombian, Lavender, Silver, White, Buff, and Red varieties.

It is said that the Pekin was liberated from the Emperor Xianfeng of China. They arrived in the British Isles sometime between 1830 and 1840 and were presented to Queen Victoria in the mid-nineteenth century. More recently, in the United States, they were crossed with the Cochin to develop and improve the breed, resulting in the Pekin bantam of today. The Pekin is not the greatest egg layer in the world, producing around ninety creamy-white eggs a year, but the breed is small and cannot sit on large quantities of eggs.

The Pekin must be kept clean and dry. In wet weather mud sticking to the leg and feet feathers makes walking difficult, and if the mud is allowed to dry and harden, it is difficult to remove. This delightful little bird is an excellent choice for a first-time owner or for children, being docile and loving company. If handled from young, the bird will happily sit on your lap. The Pekin is a true bantam; it has no large fowl equivalent.

The Pekin originated in the United States but is now found throughout the British Isles and most major continents.

Plymouth Rock

Characteristics

Barred

Color: White with blue tinge and beetle-green bars; feathers have black tip.

Also Black, Buff, Columbian, White, Silver Penciled, and less common Partridge varieties.

This beautifully feathered bird was developed in New England in the United States during the mid-nineteenth century. Many breeders claim to have developed the Plymouth Rock, but the honor has been given to John C. Bennett (1804–1867) who was involved in the development and popularizing of the breed that, prior to World War II, was the most popular in the United States. The Barred was the first on the market, followed by the Black, then the White; the Buff appeared at the end of the nineteenth century. The Plymouth Rock arrived in the British Isles in the early 1870s, and breeders immediately started to improve its exhibition qualities. Today's Plymouth Rock is a result of crosses of the Dominique, Cochin, and Black Java, with a touch of Malay and Dorking.

This dual-purpose breed is docile, long lived, and cold hardy, making it an ideal bird for the back garden or small farmer. The Plymouth Rock lays around 200 brown eggs a year.

The breed originated in the United States and is now found in the British Isles, Europe, Canada, and Australia.

Red Jungle Fowl

Characteristics

Color: Golden-orange head and hackle; long, curved tail dark metallic green with white tuft at base. Underbody black, upper body riot of rich orange, dark reds, and maroon.

This is not a chicken but a breed of tropical pheasant (*Gallus gallus*). Charles Darwin determined that this bird, along with the Gray Jungle Fowl, is the wild ancestor of the modern chicken. It is said that the Red Jungle Fowl was first domesticated over 5,000 years ago; archaeological evidence suggests that Jungle Fowl were being domesticated and reared for food and eggs in India 2,500 years ago. Only a short time later it could be found in Europe. During the mating season, it is said that the male will announce his presence with the traditional "cock a doodle doo."

Nest building and incubation are left entirely to the hen. The hen's less flamboyant plumage—a dull golden brown—is an effective camouflage when incubating the eggs and taking care of her young. This free-range bird is not entirely flightless and can achieve sufficient height to spend the evening safe from predators in a tree or other roost.

Originally from India, it is possible that the Red Jungle Fowl can now be found in Europe and on some Western continents.

Rhode Island Red

Characteristics

Color: Reddish-brown
to deep chocolate-red;
male can have black
or greenish-black
tail feathers.

An amazingly successful breed, and possibly one of the most recognized, it originated in Little Compton, Rhode Island, United States, at the beginning of the twentieth century, and now the State bird of Rhode Island. The breed was developed through a cross between the Asiatic Black-Red and a black-breasted Malay cock imported from the British Isles. This founding father is on display at the Smithsonian Institution; an "elegant monument" has been erected by the Rhode Island Red Club of America and is listed on the National Register of Historic Places.

This is an ideal breed if you want a small flock: nine hens are capable of laying six or seven eggs a day, depending on health and quality of life. Hardy and disease resistant, these chickens (although not recommended) can survive better than most on poor diet and housing. The Rhode Island Red is a dual-purpose breed, used more for eggs than meat: a good female can lay between 250 and 300 light to dark brown eggs per year, a good average being 170 to 200.

Originally from the United States, the breed is now found in the British Isles, Europe, and most major continents.

Scots Dumpy

Characteristics

Black

Color: Black with a green sheen.

Also Cuckoo, White, Brown, Silver, and Gold varieties.

It is said that the Scots and Picts used the Scots Dumpy (Bakies, Creepers, or Stumpies—take your pick) to raise the alarm at times of ambush. The birds' acute hearing meant that they could hear the sound of a thistle being stepped on (one reason why the thistle was adopted as the Scottish emblem). Chickens similar to the Dumpy were known to be around in Saxon times, and were recorded in York in northern England in the eleventh century. By the 1900s, the Scots Dumpy was extinct in all but name. Fortunately, Lady Violet Carnegie (of Carnegie Hall fame) brought back her small flock from her estate in Kenya to that of the Earl and Countess of Moray in Scotland, as breeding stock. It usually falls to small groups of dedicated breeders and breed club secretaries to step in and keep "at risk" and rare breeds from disappearing.

The Dumpy is best kept and happiest when free range. They have very short legs so good level ground is an asset. They make excellent mothers, are cold hardy and dual-purpose, and have been known to lay up to 200 eggs a year.

Originally from Scotland, the breed is now found in small numbers throughout the British Isles, Kenya, and the United States.

Scots Grey

Characteristics

Color: Male steel-gray with black bars, or barred, with metallic sheen. Hen similar but with larger markings and can have tartan appearance.

The Scots Grey is a very old and rare breed with a history going back to the sixteenth century when it would have been a common sight around the farms in Lanarkshire, Scotland. The Breed Club was formed in 1885.

The Scots Grey is a long-legged, erect bird that struts the yard like a toy soldier. It is an endangered breed, and there may only be 200 hens left in the British Isles. It is known for its hardiness and ability to survive in harsh conditions, and it requires plenty of space to roam, having a great ability to forage. When kept outdoors in the sunshine, the feathers on the neck and saddle tend to acquire a brassy sheen. Many are kept for purely ornamental reasons, but the Scots Grey provides quality-flavored meat and large (considering the bird's size) cream-tinted white, rich-tasting eggs.

Originally from Scotland, the breed is now found in small numbers throughout the British Isles, Australia, and Kenya.

Sebright

Characteristics

Gold

Color: Rich, deep golden-bay; each feather edged with black (lacing).

Also Silver variety.

Developed in the nineteenth century by Sir John Saunders Sebright, this is one of the oldest bantam breeds. The Seventh Sebright Baronet was Member of Parliament for Hertfordshire in southern England. Charles Darwin was a great fan of Sir John, frequently writing of his expertise in the development and improvement of animal species. The Rosecomb bantam was the basis for this striking breed, crossed with British and Polish birds and a touch of Hamburg and Nankin. Sir John eventually developed a laced bantam that would regularly breed true, the development and refinement continuing until 1952 before finally achieving the standard we know today.

This purely ornamental and delightful breed is hardy, active, skittish, and friendly, although not an easy bird to raise for the novice. The "heavy" male weighs in at 1 lb 10 oz (625 g); the eggs, in the region of 125 a year, are small and white. It will never achieve dual breed status. The Sebright is a true bantam, and has no larger fowl equivalent.

Originally from the British Isles, the breed is now found on most major continents.

Silkie

Characteristics

White

Color: White.

Also Black, Blue, Gold, Partridge, Triple Laced Partridge, Triple Laced Silver Partridge, and Bearded (standard Silkie with beard and earmuffs).

The Silkie is one of the oldest breeds of chicken. Its place of origin is most likely China, but Japan and India have also been suggested. The first known recorded details of the breed come from the thirteenth century when the Venetian adventurer Marco Polo wrote an account of a chicken with feathers like fur. The breed arrived in Europe more than 200 years ago via maritime traders on the Silk Road. These early poultry dealers sold them to buyers as a cross between a rabbit and a chicken!

The Silkie lays 100 cream-colored eggs in a good year, and does not lay during the summer months. The bird has black skin and bones (melanism), a rare—but not unique—trait. The gray-black meat is not generally acceptable to European and American palates. The bird requires little space, is calm and friendly, docile and trusting, as a result of which bullying can be a problem when housed with more aggressive breeds. The ideal first hen for children, or for keeping in a small garden.

Originally found in Asia, the Silkie is now seen in the British Isles, Europe, the United States, and most major continents.

Sumatra

Characteristics

Blue

Color: Male has very dark smoke-blue hackle, saddle, wing bow, and tail; rest of body paler.

Also Black and White varieties.

The Sumatra—usually called the Black Sumatra—is a rare bird; the Blue even more so. The breed comes from Angers Point, Sumatra in Indonesia and was introduced first into the United States in 1847. Frederick R. Eaton, from Norwich, introduced them to the British Isles in 1907. Exceedingly rare and extraordinarily beautiful, with a long, sweeping black tail and the elegance of a peacock, the Sumatra is now kept as a purely ornamental breed. Before reaching the United States, it was used in cockfighting, and the males frequently have the spurs to prove it. The breed has remained pure and untainted by development and improvement since its arrival in the Western world.

The Sumatra lays in the region of 120 white eggs a year and is not weighty enough to be a meat bird, so is kept purely for its stunning looks: it is the perfect exhibition bird. The breed will not tolerate confinement; the more space and the higher the trees in which to roost the happier the birds will be.

Originally from Sumatra, the breed is now found in the British Isles, the United States, and most major continents.

Sussex

Characteristics

Speckled

Color: Head, neck, and body dark mahogany; feathers have small white spot at tip with black bar above. Tail feathers black and brown with white tip.

The Sussex, from the county of the same name in southern England, is a very old breed. The Speckled is the oldest variety, although not mentioned in the Standards Book until 1865; the Sussex Club was formed in 1903. One school of thought suggests that the Old English Game bird was the starting point for the Sussex, but proof is difficult to find.

This superb dual-purpose breed was once one of the main daily sources of meat and eggs for London, a commercial venture centered on Tunbridge Wells and Eastbourne. The Light Sussex is still the principal commercial chicken, having been crossed with the Rhode Island Red, Indian Game, and the Leghorn to produce superb-quality meat. The Sussex will lay around 260 eggs a year. The Red and Brown varieties are now quite rare as is the Coronation, which was bred to celebrate the coronation of King George VI. The birds are good foragers and can adapt to most surroundings.

Originally found only in Sussex, the breed is now seen throughout the British Isles as well as in Europe, Canada, and the United States.

Wyandotte

Characteristics

Blue Laced

Color: Feathers reddish-brown with blue lacing.

Also White, Blue, Buff, Red, Black, Barred, Silver Penciled, Columbian, Partridge, Blue Partridge, Silver Laced, Gold Laced, and Buff Laced (seventeen varieties).

The Wyandotte originated in New York State and Wisconsin in the United States and was named after the Native American Indian tribe the Wyandot—also known as the Huron—and first recorded in 1873. The history of this comparatively modern breed is remarkably vague; it is a cross between a Cochin, Silver Spangled Hamburg, and "AN Other." The Silver variety was the first, resulting from a cross between the Silver Spangled Hamburg and Cochin, but did not meet with the approval of the American Standards Committee (ASC). Further development, improvements, and refinements continued until 1883, when the Wyandotte was approved by the ASC.

Often called the "bird of curves," the Wyandotte is an excellent mother, calm and docile, and has the ability to adapt to free range or smaller garden runs. With so many beautiful varieties, it is a superb dual-purpose breed, suitable for farm or show, and will lay up to 200 light to dark brown eggs a year.

Originally from the United States, the breed is now found in the British Isles and on most major continents.

COWS

Milk comes in bottles and cartons from the supermarket. Everybody knows that. When a group of children on a school trip were taken into a milking parlor one time, they were amazed and shocked in equal proportion. Years of belief gone in a flash.

Around the world, many different breeds of cattle can be found. Some have travelled far from their origins in the British Isles and Europe—where their history can be traced back hundreds, if not thousands, of years—and can now be seen in the United States and Australia. Several breeds have been developed over the years by dedicated breeders intent on producing quality stock. Others have remained untouched: the purity of the Jersey breed, for example, is jealously guarded, unlike that of the black-and-white Holstein and its Friesian cousin; it would take the likes of Sherlock Holmes to unravel their complex relationship.

Many breeds have their own society or association, and I have tried with their help to give you a glimpse of the tremendous diversity of cattle found around the globe. Some breeds are as rare as the Giant Panda, others are more numerous—but all need our protection and support.

Aberdeen Angus

Characteristics

Native color black, but red does occur.

Naturally polled.

A breed of cattle similar to the Aberdeen Angus (also known as just Angus) has been grazing the fields of Scotland since the 1500s. The breed originated with hornless cattle (known as "Hummlies" and "Doddies") in the counties of Aberdeen and Angus in northeast Scotland in the early nineteenth century. Hugh Watson, a tenant of Keillor Farm in Angus, bought quality stock from far and near and used only the finest polled black animals for breeding. In 1842, Old Jock, his favorite bull, was born. Another star of Watson's herd was a cow called Old Granny, born in 1824. She is said to have lived for thirty-five years and given birth to twenty-nine calves. Most of today's Aberdeen Angus can trace their parents back to these two animals.

William McCombie, a farmer, founded a herd based on Keillor stock and produced outstanding cattle that he showed in England and France, helping to establish the breed's reputation for quality beef. Sir George Macpherson-Grant returned to his inherited estate in 1861 and spent the next fifty years refining the Angus. Further developments and improvements continued into the twentieth century.

The Aberdeen Angus is now found throughout the British Isles and the world.

Ayrshire

Characteristics

Any shade of red
and brown, including
mahogany and white;
spots are jagged at
edges and cover the
entire body.

Elegant horns, curving
upward, outward,
and backward.

This breed originated in southwest Scotland, and was created by crossing Teeswater and Channel Island cattle. It was known initially as the Dunlop and then the Cunningham before becoming the Ayrshire, and by 1812 was an established breed. It was first officially recorded in the 1870s, and the Ayrshire Cattle Breed Society was formed in 1877. For many years the curving 12-inch-plus (30-centimeter) horns were the hallmark of the breed, a magnificent sight when highly polished for the show ring. In modern farming, horns are impractical, and today most Ayrshire cattle are dehorned as calves.

The Ayrshire is an effective grazer, enabling it to survive in less-than-ideal conditions, and a strong healthy, long-lived animal. It can survive the heat of Africa and the extreme cold of Scandinavia and still produce world-quality milk, ideal for making yogurt, cheese, and ice cream.

Originating from the county of Ayr in Scotland, there are now herds throughout the British Isles and on most continents.

Belted Galloway

Characteristics

Black, red or dun, with a white belt around the middle.

Naturally polled.

The Belted Galloway, found throughout the British Isles, is currently one of the "in favor" breeds and has experienced a tremendous upsurge in popularity. In addition to its unique appearance and the quality of the product, it is a tough, hardy, yet good-natured breed.

The origins of the "Beltie" appear to lie in the crossing of the ancient Galloway that originated in the Kirkcudbright and Wigtown areas of Scotland, and the Dutch Lakenvelder (the latter introducing the characteristic white belt). In the seventeenth and eighteenth centuries, there was an upsurge in trade with the Low Countries and the rest of the British Isles. Miss Flora Stuart of Mochrum, near Wigtown, Scotland, initiated developments that helped secure the Scottish beef industry. The health-conscious will be pleased to learn that the Galloway has the same fat content as chicken and fish.

The Belties are double-coated, with a soft short undercoat and a long shaggy overcoat that is shed in hot weather. The double coat is ideal insulation against heat loss and a good raincoat. In 1921, the Dun and Belted Cattle Breeders Association was formed and established lucrative export markets in the United States, Canada, Australia, New Zealand, Europe, and Africa.

Black Welsh

Characteristics

Varies from jet black to rusty black, but occasionally red.

Either horned or polled.

A native British breed descended from black cattle that grazed the rough mountains and hills of Wales before the Roman invasion, and possibly from cattle from the Iberian Peninsula. The modern-day Black Welsh is the result of ninety years of careful selection and breeding of two Welsh breeds: the North Wales type (raised in the hilly and mountainous regions) and the South Wales type (from a lower and gentler landscape). The Black Welsh is therefore a true British breed and possibly the oldest and purest breed in the world.

It is hardy and adaptable, growing a thick coat in winter, enabling it to graze in snow and rain when most other breeds would head for cover. It is happy grazing in the lowland areas or foraging in the uplands. This adaptability enables the Black Welsh to survive when many other breeds would starve.

Originally from Wales, the breed is now found throughout the British Isles and on most continents.

British Bazadaise

Characteristics

Light gray and slightly shaded in a wheat color; bulls dark gray with a lighter saddle.

Traditionally horned.

The Bazadaise (pronounced "baz-a-day") originated in southwest France in the Middle Ages by the crossing of a Marini, a small local gray cow, with breeds brought in from Spain by the Moors. The Bazadaise is able to work in extreme conditions from the lowlands to the Hautes-Pyrénées, a mountainous landscape bordering France and Spain. An exceptionally tough and vigorous animal, it will graze in both the extreme cold of the high alpine meadows and the heat of the Spanish border region. In France, the Bazadaise has achieved the Coveted "Label Rouge," a confirmation of its quality. Farm mechanization and war led to a decline in numbers.

In 1989, the Bazadaise was imported into the British Isles where the breed has steadily grown in popularity and is now a premier beef producer. Calm and intelligent, the Bazadaise can cope with the dry heat and aridity of Australia and the rain and cold winters of the British Isles.

Originally only found in France, the breed has spread to the British Isles, Australia, Belgium, Spain, and the Netherlands.

British Blonde

Characteristics

Predominantly wheat color, but range from almost white to brown.

The majority are horned, but there is a polled variety.

Three strains of cattle have been used to develop the Blonde: the Garonnais, the Quercy, and the Blonde de Pyrénées. The Blonde d'Aquitaine (as the breed is known on the continent) has been grazing European pastures since the sixth century—and any breed that can survive for 1,500 years must have something going for it! They were originally used as draft animals, and this continued until the end of World War II. The breed was "improved" by crossing with the Charolais and Shorthorn, but this was not entirely successful, and the Blonde was bred back to its original type.

In 1974, the breed was introduced into the British Isles. The British Blonde is a strong, hardy, lean, and docile animal. It is renowned for its lean, low fat meat qualities, leading to an increase in popularity among the health-conscious in Europe and the British Isles.

Originally found in the Garonne valley and the Pyrénées Mountains in the Aquitaine district of France, there are now herds throughout the British Isles and on most major continents.

British Blue

Characteristics

Black, white, blue, or red, or any combination.

Every calf born in the UK must be dehorned within eight weeks.

The breed originated in Belgium, where it is known as the Belgian Blue. During the latter part of the nineteenth century, the breed was imported into the British Isles to improve the native stock (at that time dairy cattle). From 1920 to 1950, the market trend was for dual-purpose breeds, and over the next ten years there was a move toward breeds with greater muscle. In the 1990s, British farmers developed the breed to suit the UK market. In 2007, the cattle became promoted and recognized as the British Blue.

The British Blue is renowned for its quiet temperament and prominent double muscling, especially around the hindquarters. It is one of the most popular sires used on the dairy herd and is a popular beef cross, producing many show-winning animals.

British White

Characteristics

White with black or red points, eyelids, ears, feet, nose, and muzzle.

Naturally polled.

The modern British White is a direct descendant of the feral white cattle of the British Isles, mainly coming from Whalley Abbey in Lancashire, owned by Richard Assheton in 1553. Almost seventy years later, Mary Assheton, heir to Middleton Hall near Manchester, married Lord Suffield and moved to Gunton Hall in Norfolk, taking with her polled white cattle from the original Whalley Abbey herd. This was the start of two major herds of British White cattle.

In 1865, rinderpest (cattle plague) almost wiped out the British White, along with many other breeds; the precautions taken at that time were the forerunner of those taken 136 years later for foot and mouth disease. It was a constant battle to maintain, let alone increase, numbers. In 1973, the Rare Breeds Survival Trust, along with increased efforts from the British White Cattle Society, ensured the survival of this beautiful animal. In 1996, the regulations were "adjusted" to limit the introduction of non-British Whites, ensuring that the breed remains true to type.

The breed was originally only found in the British Isles but is now in Australia and the United States.

Brown Swiss

Characteristics

Very pale brown to almost chocolate, with creamy white muzzle and dark nose and dark blue eyes.

When horned, horns are short and white, growing darker towards the tips.

It is agreed the Brown Swiss (or Braunvieh) is the oldest of all dairy cattle. These handsome brown cattle originated in northeastern Switzerland; skeletal remains, similar to the Brown Swiss, have been found in lakeside settlements that are thought to date back to 4000 BC. The Brown Swiss dairy cattle were developed from the Braunvieh dual-purpose cattle. The best milk-producing Braunvieh were selected and through programs to improve the breed the Brown Swiss was created. Switzerland has a reputation for producing quality cheeses, and in the summer months the cattle are moved to the mountains to graze on the sweet pastures that result from the heavy annual rainfall. The Brown Swiss is the second largest dairy breed in the world, with over fourteen million head.

Originating in the Swiss canton of Schwyz, small herds can now be found throughout the British Isles as well as in Europe, the United States, South America, Canada, Australia, South Africa, and New Zealand.

Charolais

Characteristics

Creamy white to tan with pink muzzle and pale hooves; also red or black varieties.

Traditionally horned.

White cattle were grazing in the Charolles region of France in AD 878 and were known in the markets of Lyon and Villefranche. As with most continental cattle, the Charolais was a multipurpose beast, used as a draft animal, for milk and food, and was bred for utility, not beauty. It took the French Revolution to give the breed wider popularity. In 1773, Claude Mathieu, a farmer in Charolles, moved with his white cattle to Nievre in the region of Bourgogne (also famed for its white wine). He improved the breed and it flourished to such an extent that it became known, for a short while, as the Nievmas rather than the Charolais. After World War II, the breed began to be exported to other parts of the world, first to Brazil, followed by Argentina and South Africa, and in the late 1950s, it became the first continental breed to be imported into the British Isles. The Charolais is one of the world's finest beef cattle.

The Charolais is mainly found in the United States and Europe, but has been exported throughout the world.

Devon

Characteristics

Red, varying from a deep rich to a slightly lighter color.

Naturally horned, but polling has been introduced over the years.

The Devon is also called the North Devon (and the Red Ruby) to distinguish it from the South Devon (a different breed). It is believed by some authorities that the Devon is descended from a breed of small prehistoric aboriginal British cattle, the Longifrons and the Urus, and native Devon cattle. Red cattle have grazed the hills of this part of southwestern England for centuries, and the Romans mentioned their presence in AD 55. There is also evidence that the Phoenicians brought red ancestral stock from North Africa or the Middle East to these shores on their frequent visits to buy tin. Could this be the reason why the Devon is adaptable to hot climates, despite enduring centuries of British weather? In 1623, 131 years after Columbus discovered America, the Devon were grazing in the New World. The ship *Charity* delivered one bull and three heifers to the Plymouth Colony in New England: the first purebred cattle to reach America.

Originally only found in Devon, Somerset, Cornwall, and Dorset, herds are now found throughout the British Isles, and in Europe, the United States, Brazil, Australia, and New Zealand.

Dexter

Characteristics

Predominantly black, but also red and dun.

Most are horned, but the polled is becoming more easily available.

It is frequently said that the Dexter is a comparatively new breed, but this is rubbish: this dual-purpose breed has been around for over 300 years. It was developed by careful selection of the hardy mountain breeds, descendants of the black cattle of the early Celts, by Mr. Dexter, agent to Lord Howarden who settled in County Tipperary in Ireland in 1750. It was further described in a report on Irish cattle in 1845; therefore, it is hardly a new kid on the block. The Dexter was introduced into the British Isles in 1882 by Mr. Martin of Oxfordshire and by 1892 was well established.

A small, gentle animal, 35 inches (91 centimeters) to the top of the back, it is a specialist at browsing low-quality vegetation. The Dexter produces much-sought-after quality meat and the milk is relatively high in butterfat (4 percent). In the early twentieth century, the Dexter was the show cattle of the gentry, but by 1970 the breed was rare and endangered. It was their popularity with smallholders that saw a dramatic increase in their numbers and saved them from extinction.

Originally found in south-central Ireland, there are now herds throughout the British Isles and on most continents.

Friesian

Characteristics

Predominantly black pied, but red pied in small numbers.

Can be horned or polled.

The origins of the Friesian are unclear. Small black-and-white and red-and-white cattle were brought to northern Holland and Friesland from Jutland, and crossed with Dutch cattle, so creating the basis of the modern Friesian. Its dairy qualities were recognized 2,000 years ago. The preference for the black pied resulted in breeding in favor of this color, but the red pied still exists in small numbers in the Netherlands.

The Friesians were imported into the east coast ports of the British Isles, but this was halted in 1892 to prevent the spread of foot and mouth disease, which was endemic in Europe. The Friesian of today is 75 percent Holstein, but there is an increasing use of British Friesian genetics as the benefits of the breed are currently more appreciated. The Friesian was bred for many years as a dual-purpose breed, and is now top of the list of milk-producing breeds.

Originally from northern Holland and Friesland, the breed is now found throughout the world.

Galloway

Characteristics

Predominantly black; the long outer coat can have a chestnut tinge, though dun and a small number of reds can be seen.

Naturally polled.

The Galloway is one of the oldest and purest native cattle breeds. Records show that in the sixteenth century the native cattle of southwest Scotland were producing top-quality beef; in the 1800s, thousands of Galloway were being driven south to markets in Norfolk and Suffolk.

It is an extremely hardy breed, able to survive grazing wild upland countryside, browsing on natural grass. Being double coated, with a soft downy undercoat and a long oily overcoat, it is able to survive and calve in the harshest of climates. The cross of the Galloway and the Whitebred Shorthorn is a Blue Grey; the female is crossed with European bulls to produce excellent quality beef. Foot and mouth disease in southwest Scotland, Cumbria, and Devon in 2001 decimated the oldest and leading herd breeding stock, and only the dedication and hard work of the breeders has put the Galloway once more at the forefront of British cattle.

Herds are found throughout the British Isles as well as in Russia, Canada, the United States, South Africa, Australia, and Alaska.

Gelbvieh

Characteristics

Desired color is yellow, but black Gelbvieh are on the increase.

Usually polled.

The Gelbvieh (translating as "yellow cattle," pronounced "gel-fee") originated in northern Bavaria in southern Germany at the turn of the eighteenth century and is one of the oldest German cattle breeds. It developed from a range of local red-yellow cattle, described by one enthusiast as being "golden honey red." In the late nineteenth century, this popular breed was used for food, milk, and as a draft animal. In the mid-twentieth century, red Danish cattle were introduced to improve milk production.

These quiet, docile animals are excellent mothers. Though a large animal, the calves are unusually small, resulting in fewer calving problems than with similar European breeds. The Gelbvieh is noted for the quality of its milk. The breed was imported into the British Isles in 1973 and has grown steadily in popularity. In the mid-1970s, it was biologically exported to the United States, and around this time it also arrived in Australia. It is now found in New Zealand, Canada, South America, and South Africa.

Guernsey

Characteristics

Red or fawn (wheat colored): may be pied, red, and white or fawn and white.

Usually horned.

There are many fanciful theories as to the origins of the Guernsey cow. The most common, as yet unproven, is that in AD 960 Robert, Duke of Normandy, sent a group of militant monks to defend the island of Guernsey against buccaneers and pirates, to cultivate the soil and educate the natives. They brought with them Alderney cattle from the province of Isigny, and the Froment du Leon from Brittany, and developed the Guernsey. In 1700, the Guernsey was first recorded as a separate breed, and in 1789, the import of foreign cattle was made illegal to maintain its purity.

It is renowned for the quality and the quantity of its milk and the possible health-giving properties: protection against Type 1 diabetes, autism, and maybe heart disease. The milk is richer in calcium than any other and is high in beta carotene and vitamin A that is said to prevent a number of diseases, including cystic fibrosis and arthritis, and which also gives the milk its rich golden color.

Originally from Guernsey, a small island in the English Channel off the coast of France, there are now herds throughout the British Isles, the United States, and South America, Australasia, and Africa.

Hereford

Characteristics

Dark red with white face and crest, with distinguishing white markings including crest, brisket, legs, and tail.

Two strains: horned and polled.

The origins of the Hereford go back to time immemorial. It started life as a draft ox, pulling plows, carts, and sleds. A descendant of the small red cattle of Roman Britain crossed with a large Welsh breed that grazed the borders of Wales and England, it took its name from the county in which it evolved. Numerous authors in the county of Herefordshire recorded the breed in the early seventeenth century. In 1742, Benjamin Tomkins, with two cows and a bull calf from his father's estate, produced what is accepted as the beginning of the true Hereford breed. The early breeders created the superb beef qualities that are still apparent today. The Hereford was the first English cattle to be recognized as a true breed.

This tough breed can be found in the Arctic snows of Finland, the heat of South Africa, and subtropical South America, as well as throughout the British Isles, Australasia, Europe, and the United States.

Highland

Characteristics

Black, red, yellow, brindle, or dun.

Long, sweeping horns.

Highland cattle have grazed the Scottish Highlands and islands in areas close to the Arctic Circle for more than 1,500 years. There is speculation as to how they came to be there, and being introduced by the Vikings is the most likely answer. Its undercoat and 6-inch (15-centimeter) long oily overcoat give the animal protection against the severe cold, snow, torrential rainfall, and strong- to gale-force winds. No other breed of cattle has such a superb coat; the Highland can be found happily grazing high in the Andes. This is why the meat tends to be leaner and more tender, and why they are considered dual-purpose animals as they also produce a high-quality milk. For hundreds of years, this tough breed has provided food and drink for subsistence farmers in the Scottish Highlands. The breed has played a major role in the development of the area.

Originally only from the Highlands and Western Isles of Scotland, the breed is now seen throughout the British Isles and on most major continents.

Holstein

Characteristics

Patterns of black and white.

Can be horned or polled.

This breed originated in the Netherlands around 2,000 years ago, when black cattle from Batavia and white cattle from Holland were crossed, producing a large, stylish animal with strong black and white markings. The Holstein as we know it began in the mid-nineteenth century in the United States with the import of a bull and four heifers from the Netherlands. The breed arrived in the British Isles in the late nineteenth century; between then and 1930, approximately 2,000 in-calf heifers were imported from the Netherlands, along with several bulls. After World War II, a further 200 animals were imported from Canada, including three yearling bulls, a gift from Canadian breeders. The herds graze the fields during the summer months and are fed maize and silage (made from grass) during the winter.

The average Holstein will produce approximately 15,800 pints (9,000 liters) of milk a year. Possibly the most famous Holstein was Pauline Wayne, a pet cow that grazed the White House lawns from 1910 to 1913, providing President Howard Taft and his family with milk.

The Holstein is found on most major continents.

Irish Moiled

Characteristics

Predominantly red or roan with white dorsal line, flinching, tail and underparts, dark eyebrows, and pink-gray muzzle.

Naturally polled.

Originating in northwest Ireland, this is the rarest and most distinctive cattle breed in the British Isles, and the only surviving domestic livestock native to Northern Ireland. *Moile* is Gaelic for "little round or mound" and refers to the rounded top of the animal's head. The "Moily" is a very ancient breed, its origins possibly credited to the Viking invaders of the eighth and ninth centuries.

The breed is valued for quality milk and beef production on family farms in Ireland. This quality is achieved by traditional methods, allowing the Moilys to graze on their natural food, grass: a slow and gentle process where quality of the product is more important than quantity. These fine qualities have pulled the Irish Moiled back from the verge of extinction. In 1970, only twelve remained but now there are 1,000: a great improvement, but still a long way short of assured survival. They are generally known as a docile breed and will produce a calf every year.

The Irish Moiled is found throughout the British Isles and Ireland.

Jersey

Characteristics

Usually shades of fawn and cream, although darker shades are common; black nose with an almost white border.

Traditionally horned, horns being thin and curved.

There is only one breed of cattle on the island of Jersey, and to maintain its integrity, cattle imports are banned, and have been for 150 years. The Jersey's ancestors are the Guernsey and the breeds found on the Normandy and Breton coasts that arrived in Europe from the Middle East. The Jersey has been in the British Isles for 300 years, and in its early days was called the Alderney; Her Majesty the Queen has one of the oldest herds in the country at Windsor. There is another 100-year-old herd at Osberton in Nottinghamshire, and a similar one at Birthstone on the Isle of Wight. The Jersey was exported to the United States in the mid-nineteenth century.

Jersey milk is noted for its quality rather than quantity; it is high in protein, minerals, and trace elements. Its rich natural color is derived from carotene extracted from grass, the cows' natural food.

Originally found only on Jersey, the largest of the Channel Islands off the north coast of France, there are now herds across the British Isles, Australia, Canada, Denmark, New Zealand, the United States, and Zimbabwe.

Kerry

Characteristics

Solid black with a little bit of white on the udder.

Black-tipped white horns (some are de-horned as calves).

The Kerry, which still grazes the pastures of southwestern Ireland, is a descendant of the Celtic Shorthorn, brought to Ireland by people from the Mediterranean in Neolithic times. Historians believe this to be a descendant of the Heren, a small black cattle breed that survives in the Alps, and the bulls of the Camargue. The Kerry is acknowledged as being the oldest breed in Europe and is further acknowledged as the first breed developed primarily as a milk producer. The milk is of high quality and ideal for making cheese and yogurt. The Kerry is a manageable size, long-lived, and hardy, and will remain healthy even on poor-quality grazing. They make ideal "house cows"; one cow will provide sufficient milk for the average household and rear several calves.

The Kerry became extinct on the British mainland in 1966 but was re-imported in the late 1970s. The breed is rare, but through excellent promotion is growing in number.

The Kerry is found in the British Isles and is now also in Canada and the United States.

Limousin

Characteristics

Mainly golden-red, lighter under stomach, around eyes, and muzzle. Black Limousin born light fawn or brown and darken with age, the black coats tinged with brown.

Either horned or polled; horns are fine and point forward.

Cave paintings at Lascaux near Montignac in France depict cattle very similar to the Limousin, making the breed an estimated 20,000 years old. The region in which the Limousin evolved is harsh and wet, therefore not ideal for cultivation, so farming revolved around animals rather than growing crops. As a result, the Limousin is a sturdy, adaptable, and healthy breed. Being bred in a relatively remote area, the cattle developed without interference from other breeds. In the seventeenth century, records show that the Limousin was being bred primarily as a draft animal and for food.

In early 1971, 179 purebred bulls and heifers were landed at Leith Docks in Edinburgh, Scotland, and within fifteen years it became the main beef-producing animal in the British Isles, a record it holds to this day.

Originally only found west of the Central Massif in France, the breed is now seen throughout the British Isles and on most major continents.

Lincoln Red

Characteristics

Deep cherry red with a pink skin. The color reduces the risk of sunburn and cancer.

Naturally polled.

As its name suggests, this breed originates from Lincolnshire, England. Records go back to the late seventeenth century, and DNA testing has proved that the Lincoln Red was introduced to the British Isles by Viking invaders between AD 449 and 600. In the late eighteenth century, the local Lincolnshire breed was crossed with the Cherry Red Durhams and York Shorthorns and breeds from herds created by Robert Bakewell, resulting in the Lincolnshire Shorthorn. In 1939, Eric Pentecost started the process of producing a breed without horns, and in 1960, the Lincoln Red Shorthorn became the Lincoln Red. In the late 1970s, the breed suffered in popularity in the face of imported continental breeds. The Lincoln Red was successfully crossed with selected European cattle to improve the breed's commercial standing; this was done with extreme care to retain the Lincoln Red characteristics. The original Lincoln Red is now under the umbrella of the Rare Breeds Survival Trust.

The Lincoln Red is found throughout the British Isles and on most continents.

Longhorn (English)

Characteristics

Red, brown, gray, brindle, and varicolored; all have a white line down the back.

Large, impressive, wide-curved horns; some are dehorned at birth.

A beautiful and ancient breed whose true origins are lost in time; there are prehistoric cave paintings depicting cattle similar to the Longhorn. The English Longhorn is entirely separate from the Texas Longhorn, whose ancestors originated in Spain.

The English Longhorn originated in the north of England. In 1700, the noted Robert Bakewell put his exceptional skills to developing the Longhorn. His skills in developing sheep and horses are well documented, and the results of his work on the Longhorn are still visible today. All animals are bred to suit contemporary needs, and the creamy white horns were in great demand for quality buttons, cups, cutlery handles, and lamps. When leaner meat was demanded and other materials were used for buttons and handles, the Shorthorn took over and by the nineteenth century the Longhorn's reign had ended. The decline continued for 200 years and the Rare Breeds Survival Trust prevented extinction. The Longhorn is now safe and produces quality healthy beef from eating its natural food, grass.

Originally found in northwest and central England and Ireland, there are now small herds throughout the British Isles.

Luing

Characteristics

Red-brown or dun, with medium-length hair.

Polled.

The Luing (pronounced "ling") originated on the Isle of Luing off the west coast of Scotland. The Luing is the result of skillful breed development by the Cadzow brothers—Ralph, Denis and Shane—in 1947 using the finest Shorthorn x Highland heifers and an outstanding Shorthorn bull. It was developed through necessity and economic need, and was the first new breed of cattle to be developed in the British Isles for more than 100 years. The aim was to produce a quality beef calf able to withstand the rigors of a harsh west coast Scottish winter and survive high rainfall and poor-quality grazing, as well as to return a profit. The Luing, with its heavy winter coat, does not need as much to eat to stay warm; the winter coat is shed in summer.

In 1965, the British Government recognized the Luing as a breed in its own right, and over the following years the breed was exported to all major continents. This beautiful animal is strong, healthy, easily handled, and can live for up to twenty years—exceptional for cattle.

Meuse Rhine Issel

Characteristics

Red and white.

Very short horns.

The Meuse Rhine Issel, usually called the "MRI," was developed in the Netherlands in the nineteenth century on the banks of three rivers (from where the name originates): the Maas, the Rhine, and the Ijssel. In Germany, it comes from the region of Westphalia, Rhineland, and Schleswig Holstein. For thirty years from 1920, Denmark, Luxembourg, France, and Belgium created their own red-and-white cattle using Dutch and German stock.

Originally the MRI was bred as a dual-purpose animal for food and milk, but many farmers have quite recently gone entirely into milk production. The milk is high in the protein kappa casein-B, which is ideal for producing high-quality cheese; its high protein levels also make it perfect for ice cream. The MRI was first imported into the British Isles in 1970, and there are now around 31,500 animals in the country. The breed is strong, docile, and long-lived and, apart from its high milk yield, it also produces top-quality meat.

Originally found in the Netherlands and Germany, the MRI is now found throughout the British Isles, Australia, and the United States.

Murray Grey

Characteristics

Dark skin with dark gray to light gray coat.

Naturally polled.

The Murray Grey was bred by chance in Australia. The first gray calves were an embarrassment when they appeared in a herd of black Aberdeen Angus cattle in the early twentieth century on the Peter Sutherland farm in Thologolong on the New South Wales-Victoria border, and were far from popular. But the unwanted gray cattle grew quickly and were efficient at turning grass into meat. Local farmers were soon taking notice of their growth and quality and began developing the breed. By the mid-twentieth century, the Murray Grey was a commercial success. The growth of the breed in Australia was unprecedented; the high quality was in great demand in Japan and Korea.

The Murray Grey was first imported into the British Isles in 1970 and initially struggled to find favor in the face of competition with continental cattle being imported at the same time.

Originally from the upper Murray valley in Australia, the breed is now found throughout Australia, the British Isles, New Zealand, and the United States.

Parthenais

Characteristics

Light tan to ginger-red; soft dark eyes, black nose, hooves, and ear tips.

Horned; dehorned soon after birth.

The Parthenais ("par-te-na") is one of the oldest breeds in France. The breed originated on the borders of Brittany, and the herd book dates back to 1893. The Parthenais was used as a draft animal pulling plows and carts, but it was also used for milk and beef. It is a strong, healthy, adaptable animal with the ability to survive in extremes of climate and all farming systems from intensive to ranch grazing. The calves are dehorned shortly after birth to avoid damaging each other as they grow.

The Parthenais was introduced into the British Isles in 1988–1989 and has grown steadily in popularity. For the health-conscious, the Parthenais produces excellent quality, low-cholesterol lean meat. The high-quality milk can be used to make superb butter.

Originally from the region of Parthenay in the French mid-west, it is now found throughout the British Isles, the United States, and Canada.

Piemontese

Characteristics

White or light gray, newly born calves are golden brown but within months turn white or light gray. Older bulls become dark gray with dark patches on head and neck.

Traditionally horned; the female's horns are shorter than the male's.

The Piemontese is a truly ancient breed. Archaeological evidence, including fossil remains and rock paintings, traces its ancestors back to the auroch, which was grazing at least 10,000 years ago, thus putting the Piemontese at the forefront of domestic cattle breeds. About 25,000–30,000 years ago, another breed, the Zebu, migrated west from what is now western Pakistan. Its onward journey was blocked by the Alps. This forced settlement eventually led to interbreeding between the auroch and the Zebu, and over time the Piemontese evolved in the harsh mountain terrain. Piemonte translates to "at the foot of the valley" (in this case, the Alps).

The breed is calm and friendly, a very desirable trait for farmers. In 1988, a little further down the historical road, the breed arrived in the British Isles. For the health-conscious, the meat has exceedingly low cholesterol content.

Originally from the Piemonte region of northwest Italy, there are now herds throughout the British Isles and Europe.

Red Poll

Characteristics

Dark red "conker" color with no white markings apart from the switch of the tail.

Naturally polled.

The Red Poll is the result of crossing two ancient, and now extinct, breeds—the Norfolk Red and the Suffolk Dun—in the early nineteenth century by James Reeve, a tenant farmer of the Holkham estate and a relative of Richard England. The Norfolk was the horned beef breed, and the Suffolk a polled dairy breed, whose history goes back to the Roman occupation of Britain. The result was a naturally polled, dual-purpose breed producing milk and beef of superb quality. The Red Poll is hardy and long-lived, an economical breed not requiring large amounts of food to remain healthy and sometimes used for conservation grazing. In the mid-twentieth century, numbers went into a serious decline and the breed was classified as rare. The dedication of the breeders has reversed this trend, and the breed is once more taking its rightful place in commercial farming. The year 2008 marked its 200th anniversary.

Originally from Suffolk in East Anglia, England, the breed is now found throughout the British Isles as well as in Australia, New Zealand, and the United States.

Shetland

Characteristics

Predominantly black and white, but red and white occur.

Distinctive short "Viking" horns, curving inward and slightly upward.

The Shetland is a truly ancient breed. Remains dating back to the Bronze Age have been found in archaeological excavations in the Shetland Islands, Scotland, and the breed is thought to be a descendant of the ancient and dangerous wild auroch cattle. The Shetland was traditionally a house or tenant farmer's cow, supplying a family with food and drink. Most farmers would have two cows, one in calf and one in milk, to ensure a regular supply. The Shetland is a calm, easy-to-handle yet hardy animal able to survive on poor-quality fodder, and when the grass is gone, the Shetland will eat seaweed and dried herring. The death of a cow would be a tragedy; the farmer and his family could die of starvation. The modern Shetland is ideal for the smallholder, her lightweight frame making her less likely to churn up good pasture in wet weather. For the health-conscious, Shetland milk has good levels of beneficial fatty acids and low levels of bad fatty acids, far better than commercial breeds.

Originally from the Shetland Islands, there are now herds throughout the British Isles.

Shorthorn

Characteristics

Red, red and white, or white and roan (the particular roan color, a mixture of red and white, is found in no other cattle breed).

Either short-horned or polled; some are naturally polled.

The Shorthorn has evolved over 200 years from the Durham and Teeswater cattle of northeast England. In the late 1700s, the brothers Charles and Robert Colling improved these two breeds using techniques developed by Robert Bakewell to improve Longhorn cattle. In 1783, Charles Colling acquired four cows named Duchess, Cherry, Strawberry, and Old Favorite. At the same time he became aware of superior calves in a local market, bred from a bull called Hubback. Colling bought the bull—a shrewd move since this led to the birth of a bull named Comet in 1804. Colling sold Comet six years later for 1,000 guineas — the first recorded 1,000-guinea bull (roughly $1,270 today).

Originally from the northeast of England, the Shorthorn is now seen throughout the British Isles and on most major continents.

Simmental

Characteristics

Varies from gold to red to white, may be evenly distributed in defined patches on white background. Head is white; sometimes a white band across the shoulders.

Either horned or polled; horns turn upward.

The Simmental originated in the Simmen valley in the Bernese Oberland in Switzerland and is now found in most areas of Europe, where it is the most numerous breed. It is also the second-most numerous breed in the world, succeeded only by the Brahman (a descendant of the Asian Zebu, an animal characterized by a large lump on the top of the shoulders). The Simmental dates back to the Middle Ages, and it is a cross between a small Swiss native and a large German breed. The breed was being exported to Italy as early as the fifteenth century; during the nineteenth century, it reached most of Eastern Europe, the Balkans, and Russia, and had arrived in South Africa by 1895. In 1970, the Simmental reached the British Isles. The Simmental is a docile, adaptable animal and is just as at home on a rural smallholding as it is in a more commercial farming operation.

Originally found in Switzerland, the breed is now seen throughout the British Isles and on most major continents.

South Devon

Characteristics

Rich medium red with copper tints; shade can vary.

Most horned, but polled animals do exist.

The South Devon, the largest of British native cattle, have grazed in the southwest of the country for over 400 years and are thought to be the descendants of the red cattle imported by the Norman invaders in 1066. Because of their size and nature, the cattle are known as "Gentle Giants"—they are docile and easily handled. The South Devon's predecessors were taken aboard the Mayflower at Plymouth and sailed to the North American colonies in 1620; they also supplied the staple needs of the Royal Navy during the Napoleonic wars. In the nineteenth and twentieth centuries, careful selection and breeding took place to make improvements to an animal that already supplied food and drink. Well into the 1800s, this powerful animal was also relied upon to pull the plow.

The breed was originally found in an area of Devon, England, known as the South Hams, before spreading north across Devon and west into Cornwall. Herds did not appear in other parts of the British Isles until the twentieth century. The South Devon is now found in Australia, New Zealand, and the United States.

Sussex

Characteristics

Smooth, dark red coat with white tail switches.

Naturally horned, but polled are also bred.

The Sussex a truly ancient breed, believed by some to have been around at the time of the Norman Conquest in 1066. It is thought to have descended from the horned red cattle that grazed the dense forests of the Weald of Sussex and Kent. They were used as draft animals for a number of years before being used for beef. The earliest mention of a purebred Sussex was in 1793 when Arthur Young gave the Sussex a glowing reference. They were noted for producing strong powerful oxen, ideal for working the heavy land, work which was eventually taken over by horses and tractors, at which time the Sussex was bred for food.

It is a placid, quiet-natured and adaptable animal with an amazing tolerance to extreme temperatures. In the coldest of winters, it grows a thick, curly coat as protection against the weather. It is also an efficient forager, able to survive and remain healthy on poor-quality grazing. It is accepted that there is an international ready market.

Originally from southeast England, it is now seen throughout the British Isles and is also found in the United States, South Africa, and Australia.

Wagyu

Characteristics

Black or red, black being the dominant color.

Horns whitish, darkening to black at the tip; straight or curving gently forward.

Wagyu: the caviar of beef. In 1976, several Wagyu ("wa" = Japanese, "gyu" = cattle) were exported to the United States for research into improving American cattle. Prior to this the export and breeding of Wagyu cattle outside Japan was forbidden, and there were no further imports into the United States until 1994. Originally, the majority of the Japanese population were Buddhist and therefore vegetarian, and the Wagyu were draft animals. In 1860, the laws regarding eating meat were repealed, yet for another 100 years the majority of the population lived on rice, seafood, and vegetables. The Shogun who ruled Japan from the late twelfth to late nineteenth centuries found their warriors became stronger if they ate meat. The Wagyu were given only the best to eat and beer to drink and were massaged three times daily.

The breed is known for its calm and peaceful temperament, which is believed to improve the quality of the exquisite meat. The latest research from Pennsylvania State University shows that eating Wagyu beef can reduce cholesterol.

Originally from Japan, the Wagyu is now found in the British Isles, Europe, the United States, and Australia.

White Park

Characteristics

White with black points, ears, muzzle, eye rims, and feet.

Elegant wide-spreading black-tipped horns.

The White Park is a rare ancient breed that has been in the British Isles for more than 2,000 years. The breed is not related to either the British White or the American White; although sharing color and appearance it is genetically entirely separate. Its nearest relatives are the Highland and Galloway cattle of Scotland. During the Middle Ages, the landed gentry kept them in enclosed parks, but as fashions changed in the late 1800s numbers dwindled, and the White Park headed toward extinction. It is said that James I enjoyed his White Park steak so much that he knighted it, thus eating the first "Sir Loin."

In 1941, under the threat of the German invasion, five cows and one bull were dispatched to Pennsylvania, reputedly on the orders of Winston Churchill. Later additions led to the establishment of White Park cattle in the United States. In 1940, two pairs were exported to Canada. Two of their offspring were transferred to the Bronx Zoo and then to the King Ranch in Texas, where they lived happily for the next forty years.

White Park cattle are now found throughout the British Isles and in the United States, Germany, Denmark, Australia, and Canada.

GOATS

Goats are a diverse range of beautiful (and sometimes rare) animals. Bucks and does, billies or nannies, are the source of many a children's story (who hasn't read the Norwegian fairy tale *The Three Billy Goats Gruff* to their children?). Goats were taken into the human fold more than 10,000 years ago and most breeds have been wandering the fields, hillsides, and mountains since time immemorial. From some we obtain fiber to create exquisite mohair and cashmere clothing. Others give us possibly more mundane (but equally important and extremely healthy) meat and milk, the latter frequently being turned into mouth-watering cheeses, bringing joy to me and a living to many farmers.

Goats are browsers and prefer unwanted brush, briar, and weeds to grass, their lips and tongues selecting only the tastiest plants. Extremely intelligent and curious, they are also experts at escaping from the most secure fields.

In addition they make excellent pets: you may look twice when you see a goat wandering through a hospital ward, nursing home, or rehabilitation center, but therapy goats "bring love, affection, laughter and calmness to people ailing in mind, body or spirit."

Note: Male goats are known as billy or buck; female goats as nanny or doe.

Anatolian Black

Characteristics

Weight: 99–198 lb
(40–90 kg)

Height: 28–40 in
(70–100 cm)

Both billies and nannies
have curved horns.

The Anatolian Black has been domesticated and bred on small farms in what is now Turkey since 700 BC. It is described as the Syrian type, with long, droopy ears and long hair.

This calm, gentle mountain breed is normally found in large herds around the Mediterranean and Aegean regions and is well adapted to survive the wild weather and sparse feed; the long, thick, hairy undercoat insulates the animal against the cold. They are occasionally brown, gray or pied, and have a tremendous tolerance to disease. They breed all the year round, feeding on grass and small pine, olive and almond saplings, and grain. If there is plenty of food available for the goats, the breeder will set up camp along with the herd.

The Anatolian Black is also a brilliant mowing machine. Some say the breed is aggressive and dangerous, but experts confirm that this is not the case. The Anatolian Black is bred for its milk and meat and for its fiber: it sheds 1 lb (0.45 kg) a year.

Angora

Characteristics

Weight: male 180–225 lb (82–102 kg), female 100–110 lb (45–50 kg)

Height: male 48 in (122 cm), female 36 in (92 cm)

Both have gently curving horns.

Goat hair or fiber has been used to make clothing for over 3,000 years. Mohair is the silky, lustrous, and hard-wearing fiber from the Angora goat, which is shorn twice a year, producing 9–11 lb (4–5 kg). Originally coming from the Himalayas, the goats were herded to Ankara by Suleiman Shah **while** fleeing from the legendary Genghis Khan. *Angora* derives from *Ankara*, and *mohair* from the Arabic *mukhayua*.

The finest mohair comes from the six-month-old kid, coarsening as the animal gets older. The main color is white, but black to gray and silver are being bred, plus reds and brown. Mohair is an all-season fiber, cozy in winter and cool in summer. Hats, scarves, socks, fleeces and suits—and I must not forget the cuddly teddy bear. Records show that the Angora, with its long, droopy ears, first reached British shores in the 1500s, but did not survive, and that the Angora owned by Queen Victoria suffered the same fate.

They set foot in Australia in the 1830s, and arrived in the United States in 1849. It was not until the 1980s that they were truly established in the British Isles.

Arapawa

Characteristics

Weight: male 130 lb
(59 kg), female 59–79 lb
(27–36 kg)

Height: male
26–30 in
(66–76 cm), female
24-28 in (61–71 cm)

Billies have flattened,
sweeping horns; the
nannies' horns are
shorter, rounder and
curve backwards.

The Arapawa arrived in New Zealand courtesy of the British explorer Captain James Cook, landing on the shores on February 2, 1773; in 1777, he presented a Maori chief with two goats. It is accepted that the Arapawa are the descendants of the Old English Milch goats. In 1970, the New Zealand Forest Service decided to cull them, bringing them to the brink of extinction, since they "believed" they were damaging ancient woodland. Local farmer Betty Rowe spent a lifetime battling on their behalf. A number were taken to safety off the island to breed elsewhere.

In 1993, goats from the Betty Rowe Sanctuary arrived in the United States, and in 2004, six arrived in the UK. There are less than 500 domesticated Arapawa worldwide. The American Livestock Conservancy believes them to be one of the rarest breeds in the world. They have short, fluffy coats with shaggy leggings. The colors vary from black, brown, tan, and fawn to creamy white and tri-colored, with black or dark brown badger stripes on the face.

Bagot

Characteristics

Weight: male 103 lb (47 kg), female 80 lb (36 kg)

Height: male 26 in (66 cm), female 23 in (58 cm)

Both have long horns, twisting and sweeping backwards.

The Bagot, possibly Britain's oldest breed of goat, is strongly believed to have been brought to these shores by the Crusaders. They were presented to Sir John Bagot in the 1380s by King Richard II in gratitude for the hospitality he had received at Blithfield Hall in Staffordshire. These semi-feral goats have browsed the parklands there for over 600 years. In World War II, the herd was found guilty of damaging vital crops and sentenced, by the War Agricultural Executive, to be destroyed. It was eventually agreed to reduce the herd to sixty, and that number was retained for the remainder of the war.

A number of black-and-white goats wander the hills of Wales; these are not Bagots but escapees from the Hall. Commercially, the Bagot has nothing to offer. The head and shoulders are black and the rest of the body is white. They are excellent conservation grazers but are bred for their beauty and rarity.

Bionda dell' Adamello

Characteristics

Weight: male 154–165 lb (70–75 kg), female 121–132 lb (55–60 kg)

Height: 29½ in (75 cm)

The Bionda dell' Adamello ("blonde mountain goat") originated in the Valle Savoir region of Lombardy in Italy, although its ancient origins—before it spread out into the neighboring valleys—are a little vague. Paintings of the breed date back to the eighteenth century, and in the mid-twentieth century, the Bionda was on the verge of extinction. Numerically, it is the most successful breed: in 1995 there were barely 100, but with the help of the farmers and the R.A.R.E. Association, the numbers have risen to over 4,000 and are continuing to improve.

It would be tempting to intensively breed the Bionda to take advantage of the increasing popularity of the smoked Fatuli and Mascarpi whey cheese made from their milk, but the Alpine breeds do not lend themselves to intensive breeding. In spring and summer they are taken up to the mountains and allowed to graze, as nature intended. They are capable of surviving in most climates. The long, fine fiber is light brown with regular patches of white, and white stripes each side of the muzzle.

Boer

Characteristics

Weight: male 240–300
lb (110–135 kg), female
200–220 lb (90–100 kg)

Height: 29½–31½ in
(75–80 cm)

The Boer (the Dutch word for *farmer*) was originally developed in South Africa in the early twentieth century. The Boer is believed to have been created using goats from the Namaqua Bushmen and the Fooku tribe and crossing and improving them with European and Indian breeds. It is the only goat breed in the world to be bred specifically for meat and in appearance is entirely different from the dairy breeds. The Boer has a short stocky body with a broad chest, and usually has short, white, smooth hair with a chestnut-brown head and floppy ears.

The Boer was imported into the British Isles in the mid- to late-1980s, and despite being bred in a warmer climate has adapted well to the vagaries of the British weather. It is now well established, and has created an excellent export market. It will quickly clear a pasture of weeds, thus improving it for grass-feeding stock.

British Alpine

Characteristics

Weight: male 170 lb
(77 kg), female 135 lb
(61 kg)

Height: male 37 in
(95 cm), female 32 in
(83 cm)

Both are horned
or polled.

There are two types of Alpine goats: the British and the French. A Swiss goat with the grand name of Sedgmore Faith at the Paris Zoo had the beautiful and distinctive black-and-white markings of her breed; in 1903 she was brought to England and crossed with a Toggenburg of similar coloring. All the kids had beautiful Swiss markings. More breeding and refining took place; the British Alpine had arrived and was here to stay, Sedgmore Faith being the grandmother of them all.

The British Alpine is tall and graceful with a short, fine, glossy black coat with white or cream facial and leg markings. The ears are erect, pointing slightly forward. An area to forage, a supply of hay and a muesli-type supplement is the key to happiness. They produce a good supply of quality, easily digestible alternative milk for all the family.

British Primitive

Characteristics

Weight: 100–200 lb
(45–54 kg)

Height: male 24–27
in (61–69 cm), female
22–24 in (55–61 cm)

The large horns form
a scimitar twist.

The British Primitive is the name that covers the breeds previously known as the Old English, the Scottish, the Welsh, the Irish, and British Landrace, not forgetting the Old British Goat. The British Primitive is a descendant of the goats bred by the farmers of the Neolithic (New Stone Age). The Vikings, Saxons, or Celts would have bred this hardy animal that was a born survivor, protecting itself and its young against predators as well as having the ability to survive the harshest of weather on a poor and meager diet. They have long, thick, dense hair, colored mainly white, gray and black.

The breed provided the farmer and his family with milk, meat, skin, and fiber for clothing, and tallow for heating and lighting. Nothing was wasted. They are now used for scrub clearance and conservation grazing.

Chamois

Characteristics

Weight: male 66–132 lb (30–60 kg), female 50–99 lb (25–45 kg)

Height: 28–30 in (71–76 cm)

Both have horns.

The beautiful Chamois originated in the Canton of Berne in Switzerland, and it is at home in the steep and rugged terrain of the Alps. This nimble, surefooted animal can reach speeds of up to 10 mph (16 kmph) in these rocky landscapes. The summer coat is reddish brown with a dark dorsal stripe; in winter the coat is blackish brown. They have a brown face with a darker stripe running from the muzzle to the eyes.

The Chamois is an ideal dairy goat and produces good quantities of sweet-tasting milk; their docile temperament makes them ideal pets (until you try to trim their hooves, when they can be quite a handful!). They are said to be brilliant bramble mowers. Milk from the Chamois is used to create the beautiful and creamy Fryberg-Chäs cheese.

Fainting

Characteristics

Weight: 80–150 lb
(36–68 kg)

Height: 17–25 in
(43–64 cm)

Both billies and nannies
usually have horns
that sweep upwards
and outwards.

In the early nineteenth century an elderly farm laborer, strangely dressed, arrived in Marshall County, Tennessee, accompanied by four goats and a cow: enter John Tinsley. Soon everyone was talking about John's goats that, if surprised or frightened, would stiffen or fall over. The condition is known as myotonia congenita: the muscles contract for a few seconds (this neither harms nor hurts the animal, which will continue to chew food already in its mouth). Before moving on, John sold his goats to Dr. H. H. Mayberry, who bred them and sold them locally. They became known as the Tennessee Fainting goats.

The Fainting goat's coat comes in many colors but mainly black and white, or red and white, and can be short to shaggy. They take up to three years to mature and make ideal pets.

Golden Guernsey

Characteristics

Weight: male 150 lb
(68 kg), female 120 lb
(54 kg)

Height: male 28 in
(71 cm), female 30 in
(66 cm)

Billies can be horned.

The origin of the breed is unknown, but research by the University of Cordoba in Spain has concluded that the breed is indigenous to the island. Even during the dark days of World War II, when for five years Guernsey was under German occupation, the breed was still being registered. The long-haired coat comes in all shades of gold from pale to bronze, sometimes with small white markings and a star on the forehead.

One of the largest and possibly best-known herds was that of Miss Milbourne of L'Ancresse who owned over fifty Golden Guernseys, which played an important part in helping revive the breed in the 1930s. The gene pool is very small and tremendous efforts are being made to improve the situation and secure the future of this beautiful breed. In an effort to safeguard their future, a number are being raised in New York State, but only the purebred with UK registration are allowed to use the proud title of "Golden Guernsey."

Icelandic

Characteristics

Weight: male
200–220 lb
(60–80 kg), female
150–161 lb (35–60 kg)

Height: male
29½–31½ in
(75–80 cm), female
25½–27½ in (65–70 cm)

Both can be horned
or polled.

The Icelandic goat is an endangered species, and there are no pure Icelandic goats outside the country. It is also called the Settlement goat, arriving in Iceland with the Norwegian settlers over 1,100 years ago, and there have been no further imports since that time. They are brown, gray, black, and white in various patterns. Under the coarse outer coat of long guard hair is a coat of high-quality cashmere that is combed out once a year, harvesting 6–8 oz (170–225 g). In 1986 six were exported to Scotland for a cashmere breeding program. They were put together with three other breeds to produce a new synthetic goat breed, the "Scottish Cashmere Goat."

In the early twentieth century, there were in the region of 3,000 goats, but by the latter end of the century, the number had plummeted to fewer than 400. The government has introduced a conservation program, and the numbers are slowly increasing. There is commercial and economic potential for the Icelandic through cashmere, milk, and meat. They are at present kept as pets.

Kiko

Characteristics

Weight: male
250–300 lb
(113–136 kg), female
100–150 lb (45–68 kg)

Height: 17–25 in
(43–64 cm)

Both have horns;
the billy's impressive
spiralling horns sweep
upwards and outwards.

The Europeans who discovered New Zealand in 1769 brought goats with them, and a number of them escaped and thrived. These goats were to become the modern Kiko, growing in number through having no natural predators. With no shelter, no supplementary feed, no veterinary care, and no help giving birth, they became a tough and hardy breed, resistant to disease, parasites, and the weather. The Kiko, Maori for "meat," became totally self-sufficient.

The breed as it is known today was developed by Garrick and Anne Batten on the South Island in the 1970s, and only the best of the best were selected. In the early 1990s, a number were imported into the United States by Dr. An Peischel, and they continued to grow in popularity. In summer the coat is smooth and shiny and usually white, although it can be colored; in winter the hair is long and flowing.

Kinder

Characteristics

Weight: male
135–150 lb (61–68
kg), female 110–125 lb
(50–75 kg)

Height: male
20–28 in (51–71
cm), female 20–26 in
(51–66 cm)

Both are horned.

The Kinder (KIN-der) is a cross between a Nubian and a Pygmy goat. On the Zederkamm Farm in Washington in 1985, the Nubian buck died leaving the owners, Pat and Art Showalter, with two Nubian females but no mate. They did not want to send the goats to another farm to mate. Pat and Art also bred Pygmy goats. Left to his own devices, the Pygmy buck accomplished two successful matings, making use of logs and rocks and the sloping land to gain the correct height. In late June 1986, three Kinder does were born, and a year later the first Kinder buck.

The coat is short, fine hair in any goat color and pattern; the longish ears stick out to the sides. The Kinder is gentle and family-friendly and makes a good pet. The milk is ideal for drinking and for making delicious yogurt and cheese.

La Mancha

Characteristics

Weight: male 150 lb
(70 kg), female 130 lb
(59 kg).

Height: male 30 in
(76.25 cm), female 28 in
(71 cm).

Both can be horned
or polled.

The first La Mancha (or Lamancha) were bred in Oregon by Mrs.
Eula Fay Frey in 1938. The two offspring, Peggy and Nesta, are the
foundation of the breed. It is also the only goat breed developed in the
United States. The breed is recognizable by its very short ears, less than
1 inch (2.5 centimeters) long. Short-eared goats, found throughout
Spain, are mentioned in ancient Persian writings, and also by the Spanish
missionaries who colonized California in the mid-eighteenth to mid-
nineteenth centuries, bringing with them short-eared goats—and it is
believed these are the ancestors of the La Mancha.

They are known for their high production of butterfat-rich milk,
which is used for making cheese, yogurt, ice cream, and soap. They have
a laid-back attitude to life, are hardy, and make superb brush and bramble
mowers. The hair is short, fine, and glossy. And what about color? Think of
any goat color or combination of colors—and that is the La Mancha.

Nigora

Characteristics

Weight: male 80–120 lb (36–55 kg), female 60–90 lb (27–41 kg)

Height: 19–29 in (48–74 cm)

Both can be horned or polled.

The Nigora is a small- to medium-size goat developed in the United States in the 1990s as a dual-purpose animal to produce quality fiber and milk. The breed is a cross between a Nigerian Dwarf buck and an Angora doe (the first doe was named Cocoa Puff of Skyview). Since then there have been gentle adjustments and improvements to the breed. It was designed with the urban hobby farmer and smallholder in mind, and its small size and relative ease of care also making it an ideal pet. The advertising blurb states, "It is a breed particularly suited for the micro-eco farming niche." The breed can be any color and markings, and has erect ears.

The fiber is classed mainly as "cashgora," a cross between cashmere and Angora. The fiber is in three types: (A) the Angora type, long and lustrous; (B) the cashgora combines mohair with the cashmere-type undercoat and is of medium length; (C) like cashmere and is shorter. What more could you ask for: quality milk and the makings of a sweater!

Nubian

Characteristics

Weight: male 175 lb
(79 kg), female 135 lb
(61 kg)

Height: male 35 in
(89 cm), female 30 in
(76 cm)

Hornless by disbudding.

The Nubian goat is also called the Anglo Nubian, but in the United States is just known as the Nubian. The breed was developed in the UK in the nineteenth century from breeds originating in the Middle East and North Africa and the Old English Milch goat. Small improvements have been carried out over the years, and the Anglo-Nubian was officially recognized as a breed in 1896. It has a short, fine, glossy coat that can be of any color or pattern, large pendulous ears, and a Roman nose.

The Nubian is also known for producing high-quality, high-butterfat milk, the "Jersey" of the dairy goat world. Being an extremely calm and affectionate breed, a pat on the head or stroking the neck will make you a new friend—they thrive in human companionship. They will bleat to call you, especially when they want food. They require plenty of roughage, branches, weeds, the occasional rose clippings, and shrubs. If you are considering keeping a Nubian, remember that "Houdini" is their middle name!

Oberhasli

Characteristics

Weight: male
143–165 lb (65–75
kg), female 99–120 lb
(45–54 kg)

Height: male 30–34 in
(75–85 kg), female
28–32 in (70–80 cm)

Both are polled.

The Oberhasli goat is a dairy breed originating in the mountainous canton of Bern in Switzerland. Oberhasli goats were first imported into North America in the early 1900s, though it was not until 1936 that purebred herds were established and maintained. The Oberhasli is alert in appearance with a friendly, quiet, and gentle disposition. While the does are a dependable source of milk, bucks and wethers are also useful as pack animals because of their strength and calm demeanor.

Oberhasli goats are brown, with hues between light tan and deep reddish brown. Two black stripes from the eyes to the black muzzle give a distinctive facial appearance. The Oberhasli has a black belly and a light gray to black udder. The legs are black below the knees, prompting the Swiss to refer to them as "booted goats." The breed is well known internationally and is relatively numerous in Switzerland.

Poitou

Characteristics

Weight: male 120–165 lb
(55–75 kg),
female 105–140 lb
(40–65 kg)

Height: male 30–35
in (75–90 cm), female
25–30 in (65–75 cm)

Both can have
curving horns.

The legend has it that the Poitou dairy goat was left on French soil by Arab warriors after their defeat in AD 732, but archaeological evidence suggests that they have been in the region for over 5,000 years. The goat we know today originated around the area of the Sevre River in the 1800s. In 1876, the crops failed and the farmers turned to dairy production to make a living. In 1906, a cooperative was formed and local cheeses entered the market. In 1920, a foot and mouth outbreak reduced the numbers. In 1985, a major local agricultural college decided to replace its herd of Poitou, creating an outcry from the local breeders who set up a protection society—and the numbers have been on the increase ever since.

Poitou goats have a distinctive appearance. They are tall, with long, shaggy hair, and black-brown with white marks on the head and neck. They are peaceful, calm, and friendly. The milk is used to produce the famous Chabichou du Poitou cheese, among others.

Pygmy

Characteristics

Weight: male 60–86 lb
(27–39 kg),
female 53–75 lb
(24–34 kg)

Height: 16–23 in
(41–58 cm)

Both are horned.

The Cameroon Dwarf goat, as the Pygmy was originally known, comes from West Africa. During the 1950s, many were imported into mainland Europe where they were exhibited in zoos as exotic animals. Within a few years they had found their way to the British Isles where they have proved very popular. They were then exported to the United States in the 1950s.

The Pygmy is hardy and adapts to most climates. They are great browsers and will clear your weeds (and no doubt your herbaceous borders). Small they may be, but they produce a large amount of milk. These goats are mainly black, white, gray, and brown in color and both sexes have horns, but only the billy has a beard. They are social animals and need a companion, not necessarily one with four legs: the Pygmy is an ideal pet for children of all ages. They enjoy climbing, having something to jump on, and living in a warm, draft-free home in the winter. Because they are gentle and affectionate, they are frequently used as therapy animals. They are not bred for meat or milk but purely as pets and for companionship.

Pygora

Characteristics

Weight: male 75–95 lb (34–43 kg), female 64–75 lb (29–34 kg)

Height: male 23 in (60 cm), female 18 in (45 cm)

Can be horned or polled.

The Pygora originated in the United States. The inspiration for this beautiful breed came from Katherine Jorgensen seeing the colored, curly goats on a visit to the Navajo Indian Reservation. The first generation, a cross of the Pygmy and Angora, created in the mid- to late-twentieth century, were all white; the colors—red, brown, black, and gray or a mixture—did not appear until the second and third generations.

Many artists use this exquisite fiber for hand- and machine-spinning, knitting, weaving, and creating tapestries. There are three types of fiber: (A) angora style, being lustrous, curly, and up to 6 inches (15 centimeters) long; (B) curly and can be lustrous or matte and 3–6 inches (7.5–15 centimeters) long; (C) cashmere style, 1–3 inches (2.5–7.5 centimeters) long, almost straight, with a matte finish. A and B are shorn twice a year; C is harvested by brushing. Most Pygora, because of their docile and friendly nature, are kept as pets.

Saanen

Characteristics

Weight: male
143– 176 lb (65–80
kg), female 121–143 lb
(55–65 kg)

Height: male 37 in
(94 cm), female 32 in
(81 cm)

Both usually have horns.

The Saanen's origins are in the Saanen valley in Switzerland. In the late nineteenth century, many thousands were rounded up for export. The breed arrived in the United States in 1904; they were also distributed throughout Europe, arriving in the British Isles via Holland in 1922.

The Saanen is the largest of the dairy goats and can produce up to 1 US gallon (4 liters) of milk a day, gaining her the title of "The Queen of Dairy Goats." Like all goats, they need a reasonable space to browse leaves and clover. They do not like getting wet, so a shelter from the rain is a must, and a warm, draft-free shelter for the winter. The hair is short and white or light cream, some having a fringe down the spine and longer hair over the tops of the legs, and the ears are erect and pointing forward. This calm, gentle, easy-to-handle animal makes an ideal pet and companion for children.

San Clemente Island

Characteristics

Weight: male and female 51–121 lb (23–25 kg)

Height: male 23½ in (60 cm), female 22½ in (56.75 cm)

Both are horned. Their large horns resemble those of the Spanish goat and flare up and outwards.

The goats were brought to the island, which lies off California, by Salvador Ramirez in 1875. The US Navy is responsible for the upkeep of the island. In 1980, there were in excess of 15,000 goats browsing there, damaging plant and animal life. The courts sent in trappers, and 3,000 were re-established off the island. Further controls were needed, and so the Navy decided to go in with helicopters and guns, but this action was blocked by the Fund for Animals.

There are now only 700 San Clemente goats. A study in 2007 found that the goat was not of Spanish origin, but a genetically distinct breed and unrelated to the numerous other breeds in the study. Coloring is light brown to dark red or amber. The head is black, with a brown stripe from around the eye to the muzzle, and a dorsal stripe down the back. These are shy, gentle creatures that make ideal pets and produce sweet-tasting milk.

Savanna

Characteristics

Weight: 200–250 lb
(91–113 kg)

Height: 19–25 in
(48–62 cm)

Billies and nannies have
black horns growing
back and downwards.

The Savanna was developed in Douglas, South Africa, in 1955 by the
Cillier family using local goats. To survive in the harsh local conditions,
the goats needed to be tough, strong, and disease- and parasite-resistant.
They needed to be able to survive extremes of heat and cold, intense
sunshine, and rain. In the cold, their fine hair grows to give added
protection. The coat is short, smooth, white hair, occasionally with
red, blue, or black "freckles." The skin is loose and black, and the ears
are floppy.

Their diet is not that of the usual farm animal: they eat large bushes,
trees, and seedpods. The main requirements to survive on this diet are
strong jaws, long-lasting teeth, and strong back legs to enable them to
reach the higher leaves and branches. If you want a breed of goat that
doesn't require a wet nurse, the Savanna is for you.

Spanish

Characteristics

Weight: male
150–200 lb
(68–91 kg), female
80–135 lb (36–61 kg)

Height: 17–25 in
(43–63.5 cm)

Both have horns; those
of the billy may be large
and twisted.

In the sixteenth century, Spanish explorers brought goats from their homeland to the Caribbean Islands, and eventually they arrived in what is now the United States and Mexico. The Spanish goat of today is the result of crossbreeding with many of the New World breeds. Until the *Mayflower* sailed from Plymouth and anchored off what became New England in 1620, the only goats in North America were the Spanish.

It is an extremely hardy breed, but unfortunately it is threatened with extinction and is on the American Livestock Breeds Conservancy watch list. Like most goats, they were originally bred for food but their other names—the Brush and Scrub goat—give a clue. Someone once wrote, "They are excellent for clearing brush and undesirable plant species from pastureland." All colors are acceptable. The hair is short, with longer hair on the lower parts of the body. The ears are long and fall to the sides of the head.

Stiefelgeiss

Characteristics

Weight: 110– 176 lb
(50–80 kg)

Height: 26½–33½ in
(67–85 cm)

The horns are thick
and curve back from
the head; the nanny's
(though similar) are
slightly smaller.

The Stiefelgeiss, or the Booted goat, is a robust and hardy breed and
well suited to life in its harsh mountain habitat. Until 1920, it could be
found in the uplands of St. Gallen in Glarus, Switzerland, but by the
1980s, the breed was on the verge of extinction, and so ProSpecieRara
took control. The Booted Goat Breeders Club of Switzerland has now
taken over management of the breed and farmers all over Switzerland
are being actively encouraged to breed the Stiefelgeiss for its milk, meat,
and fiber.

   Their appetite for leaves, buds, and bark makes them an ideal tool
to preserve the quality of pastureland. They also make ideal surrogate
mothers. Their color ranges from a light grayish brown to a dark reddish
brown. They have beards and longer hair on their back legs that is usually
a different color, hence the "boots."

Toggenburg

Characteristics

Weight: male 150-200 lb (68–91 kg), female 125 lb plus (57 kg plus)

Height: male 34–38 in (86–96.5 cm), female 30–32 in (76–81.25 cm)

Usually without horns.

They were developed 300 years ago in the Toggenburg region of St. Gallen in Switzerland and were the main source of income for the poorest families. All the Toggenburgs, called Toggs by their loving owners, were pooled and grazed on the Alpine pastures as one herd; the cheese produced from the sweet-tasting milk was distributed among the owners. The Togg was imported into the British Isles in 1822, and the following year four were exported to the United States. This robust breed has been exported to many countries, but like most Alpine breeds is happier in temperate climes.

Their medium-length coat is light fawn to the darkest chocolate; the ears are white with a dark spot in the middle and two white stripes down the face. The lower parts of the legs are white. In the *Guinness Book of World Records,* the Toggenburg owned by Lilian Sandburg of North Carolina holds the record for producing 1,140 gallons (5,182.5 liters) of milk in 365 days.

Valais Blackneck

Characteristics

Weight: male 132–198 lb
(60–90 kg),
female 99–132 lb
(45–60 kg)

Height: male 29½ in
(75 cm), female 29½ in
(75 cm)

Scimitar-shaped horns:
billy 31½ in (80 cm)
long, nanny 17¾ in
(45 cm) long.

The Valais Blackneck is a dual-purpose breed with an international reputation and is known by many names, including Col Noir de Valais and the Glacier goat. The Valais Blackneck was developed from indigenous goats crossed with the Italian Kupferziege goat and further improved by selective breeding, and are found mainly in the Lower Valais in Switzerland. This hardy breed has long, shaggy, wavy hair, white from the shoulders back; the head, neck, and front legs are black. They have the ability to tolerate the harsh winter conditions but are housed in the worst weather. It is a gourmet browser feeding only on the greenest of Alpine grass, fresh herbs, and flowers and produces up to 4¼ pints (2 liters) of milk daily.

In 1970, this protected species was close to extinction, but fortunately for this most beautiful, most photographed goat the numbers are improving, and there are now approximately 3,000.

PIGS

Pigs, hogs, or swine—whatever you like to call them—have been around for 11,000 years. Over the many centuries, they have provided humankind with food and, in earlier times, with bones for tools and weapons, skin for shields, and bristles for brushes. Those breeds that you have the most chance of seeing are included here.

Pigs are considered to have intelligence beyond that of a three-year-old child. In the last few years, numbers of this bright-eyed animal have declined dramatically and several breeds have become extinct.

Whose fault is it? To my mind, national governments, loss of habitat, the EU, and food fads must all take some of the blame, along with rules and regulations created by people who know or care little about the industry. We should not discard breeds because they are unfashionable or do not fit in with our current ways of living. Organizations such as the UK's Rare Breeds Survival Trust (RBST) and The Livestock Conservancy in the United States do what they can to protect endangered breeds, but we must all help preserve the rare and endangered animals on this fragile planet. As the T-shirt slogan tells us, extinction is forever.

American Guinea Hog

Characteristics

Weight: male/female
150–300 lb (68–136 kg)

Color: usually solid black; occasionally white points at the feet and tip of nose (due to a recessive gene). Upright ears and a curly tail.

Unique to the United States, the American guinea hog is a critically endangered breed. It was originally imported from the Canary Islands and West Africa in the seventeenth century. Having been crossed with breeds that are now extinct, it is impossible to create an accurate picture of this animal's true history. One possible ancestor is the small, black Essex pig, known to have lived in the southeastern United States where most American guinea hogs are found today.

In the early days, the breed was expected to forage for its own food—roots, grass, nuts, rodents, and even snakes. The American guinea hog is now kept on small farms and large ranches, where it keeps the area clear of vermin. The hog's friendly, docile nature is an added bonus; this tough little pig is not averse to having a good tummy rub and a back scratch.

Berkshire

Characteristics

Weight: male 617 lb
(280 kg); female 480 lb
(220 kg)

Color: black with white
socks and tip of tail;
white flash on the face.
Pricked up ears.

The Berkshire pig was "discovered" by Oliver Cromwell and his troops while spending the winter near Reading, England. A native of the British Isles, this is also reputed to be its oldest breed. It was improved in the 1700s with the introduction of Chinese and Siamese breeds. This bloodline has remained pure for more than 200 years. The original Berkshire was reddish or sandy colored and occasionally spotted. If you look closely at today's Berkshire, sand-colored hair is sometimes found hidden among the white patches. The theory is that the breed is at its best when given good food and good housing. Yet in New Zealand, where early settlers established the breed, it wanders at will and is more inclined to graze.

In the 1800s, the royal family bred Berkshire pigs at Windsor Castle and presented them to the Japanese imperial family. Pork quickly became a delicacy in Japan. In Japanese restaurants today, "kurobuta pork" comes exclusively from the Berkshire pig.

Black Iberian

Characteristics

Weight: male/female
353 lb (160 kg)

Color: completely
black or gray, including
the hooves

The Iberian pig is indigenous to the Mediterranean region, where it is the last known breed to live entirely in the open. It is thought the Phoenicians introduced the breed to the Iberian Peninsula some 3,000 years ago—originally from the eastern Mediterranean, where they had bred with wild boars.

The Black Iberian lives mainly under the cover of oak trees growing in Andalusia in southern Spain. The microclimate of the region is ideal for the oak trees' growth and consequently for the acorns that are the main food of the Black Iberian. It is a diet that gives the ham of this pig its unique flavor. Production is for quality not quantity. The Black Iberian is rare, but well regulated, with just 15 pigs allowed per 2½ acres (1 hectare). This breed has a special place in the pig world; its sheer quality has defied economics and a fickle public for centuries.

British Landrace

Characteristics

Weight:
male 500–700 lb
(226–318 kg);
female 450–600 lb
(204–272 kg)

Color: white. Long,
drooping ears.

A broad genetic base makes this pig unique among the landrace breeds throughout the world. Originally native to Sweden, the breed was imported into the UK in 1949, to be studied in an independent valuation carried out in the city of York. Subsequent imports were made for evaluation, to broaden the commercial base, and to allow further development into what was to become the British Landrace pig, now found throughout the UK, mainly in Yorkshire and the eastern counties. It is also found in Scotland and Northern Ireland.

The Landrace Breed Society joined forces with the National Pig Breeders Association in 1978, and the UK is now one of the leading breeding countries of Landrace pigs. Although it is an endangered breed, it is biologically exported worldwide—its semen is extracted by various methods, bottled, and frozen before leaving the country. The British Landrace produces excellent pork and bacon.

British Lop

Characteristics

Weight:
male 771½ lb (350 kg);
female 661¼ lb (300 kg)

Color: white. Lop ears.

Originating in the Tavistock area of Devon, the British Lop is one of the UK's largest native breeds. It is also one of the most endangered and one of a group of Celtic breeds, the rest of which are all now extinct. It is, apart from its color, very similar to the Large Black.

Originally named the Devon Lop or Cornish White in the Tavistock area, in the early years of the twentieth century the breed was also known as the Long White, Lop-Eared Pig, or the National. It was finally christened the British Lop in 1960. Initially, it spread across the southwest of the country, but seldom strayed out of this area. Now, it can be found throughout the country and also in France.

A litter is usually 12–14 piglets, and the British Lop is an excellent and docile mother. It is suited to outdoor breeding, despite the color of its skin, and with a good-quality shelter can remain outdoors year-round. The pigs need protecting against sunburn but little specialist care is needed otherwise. This breed produces excellent pork and bacon.

British Saddleback

Characteristics

Weight:
male 705½ lb (320 kg);
female 595¼ lb (270 kg)

Color: black with white saddle or band around shoulders and front legs.

The British Saddleback is native to East Anglia and the Isle of Purbeck in the British Isles. Created in 1967, it is the result of mixing two similar breeds: the Wessex Saddleback, which originated in the New Forest, and the Essex. The original Essex was improved when Lord Western crossed it with the Neapolitan. Both breeds were suffering from changes in farming practices, and the Essex was in sharp decline. Many believe that, had the Rare Breeds Survival Trust (RBST) been in existence in 1967, this amalgamation of breeds would not have taken place. There is a very small number of this breed in the United States.

Since 2007, the British Saddleback has been listed by the RBST as a minority breed. It has been exported to Nigeria and the Seychelles, where it copes extremely well with the heat and coarse grazing; its coloring protects against sunburn. The breed is to be used as part of a woodland restoration project at Haigh Hall Country Park in Greater Manchester, where it will clear nettles, brambles, and rhododendrons. The quality of the meat is superb.

Choctaw Hog

Characteristics

Weight: male
242–300 lb
(110–136 kg);
female, 150–199 lb
(68–90 kg)

Color: mainly black,
with occasional
white markings.

This hog is traditionally kept by the Choctaw Native Americans. It is a descendant of pigs the Spanish brought to the continent in the sixteenth century, and which were later bred by the Native Americans in the southeastern states. When the Choctaw moved from the Deep South to Oklahoma, they took these hogs with them. Today's hogs are direct descendants of the Oklahoma stock, and their appearance has not changed in more than 150 years.

The hogs are still reared in the traditional manner. They are earmarked and then released to run free, foraging for roots, acorns, berries, and plants. They are periodically rounded up and sorted for market, breeding, or meat, and those that are released hurtle back into the woodland with amazing agility. The Choctaw hog is extremely rare. It does not have a high profile within the food industry and is seldom written about. Money is needed to preserve this part of American history, yet sadly it is slow in coming.

Duroc

Characteristics

Weight: male
450–750 lb
(227–340 kg);
female 450–650 lb
(204–295 kg)

Color: golden-brown
to rich, red mahogany.

In 1812, pigs known as Red Hogs were bred in New York and New Jersey. In 1823, Isaac Frink of Saratoga bought from Harry Kelsey a red boar whose parents were believed to have been imported from Britain. Harry also owned a prize stallion named Duroc, and the boar was given the stallion's name. By the mid-nineteenth century, systematic crossing of the red boar's descendants with the Red Hog created the ancestors of the modern Duroc.

The breed was imported into the British Isles in the 1970s but was not an immediate success. A second import took place in the 1980s and that fared better. The Meat and Livestock Commission carried out extensive trials to assess the merits of the breed. The Duroc has since found a place in British farming and a British version of the Duroc has been developed. A thick coat enables the breed to survive the British winters, but it molts in the warmer summer months. Because of its coloring, this breed is less likely to suffer from sunburn. The Duroc produces excellent pork and bacon.

Gloucestershire Old Spot

Characteristics

Weight: male 600 lb
(272 kg); female 500 lb
(227 kg)

Color: white with
clearly defined black
spots. Large floppy ears
cover the face down to
the snout.

The Gloucestershire Old Spot is the oldest pedigree spotted pig in the world and is native to the Vale of Berkeley on the banks of the Severn River in England. The first pedigree records of pigs were made in 1885—much later than for other agricultural animals because the pig was the peasant's animal and was never highly thought of.

Also known as the Gloster Spot, The Cottager's Pig, and the Orchard Pig, this breed appears to be the result of crossing the original Gloucester with the unimproved Berkshire, a sandy-colored pig with spots. A Gloucestershire Old Spot must have one spot to qualify. Fashions change over the years from very spotty pigs to ones with very few spots at all. Old Spot is a large and docile animal, and provided it has a warm and dry shelter, it will happily spend the entire year outdoors. The breed once grazed orchards, eating windfall apples to supplement its diet, and local folklore insists the black spots are bruises from falling fruit.

Hampshire

Characteristics

Weight: male 600 lb (300 kg); female 550 lb (250 kg)

Color: black with a white belt; the belt goes across the shoulders and around the body covering the front legs. The ears are erect.

The Hampshire is thought to be the oldest American breed in existence. The original breeding pigs were imported from Wessex in the UK in 1832. In America, it was known as the Thin Rind because of the lean meat it produced. It was in 1890, at a meeting of American breeders, that it was renamed the Hampshire. This breed is used as a crossbreeding sire to improve the quality of other breeds.

The first Hampshires to arrive in the British Isles came in 1968, when they were imported by the Animal Breeding Research Organization and thoroughly tested before being made available to British breeders. In 1973, import restrictions did not allow direct imports from America, so forty carefully selected pigs were imported from Canada. In 1975, one of these became a breed champion at the English Royal Show. The Hampshire is extremely popular worldwide.

Hereford

Characteristics

Weight: male 800 lb
(362 kg); female 600 lb
(272 kg)

Color: red, with two
or more white feet.
A dished face and a
wavy tail.

R. U. Webster of La Plata, Missouri, first created Hereford hogs in 1902, by crossing the Duroc and Chester breeds. In 1920–25, John Schulte and a group of breeders in Iowa created a second Hereford breed by crossing the Duroc with the Poland China. The modern Hereford is a descendant of this second line. The breed is named for the Hereford cattle because of its similarity in color. It is docile and matures before many other breeds, and is at ease indoors or outdoors and in a wide range of climates. It also has clean habits, ensuring its bathroom is a good distance from where it eats and sleeps. This hog's digestive system is similar to that of a human, and the Hereford always chews its food to avoid stomach problems. The meat is lean and good quality.

Hybrid

Characteristics

Weight and color vary.

The hybrid is found worldwide. Used by commercial pig producers, it is created by breeding two distinct breeds or lines together to combine the best features of both parent breeds. Hybridization has been carried out for thousands of years under many different names. In recent years, sows from the Large White and Landrace breeds have traditionally been the most widely used in the UK. The pigs shown in the photograph are first-cross hybrids of Meidam and Large White, known as hybrid AC1. The benefits of hybridization include increased litter size, a greater resistance to disease, and the ability to withstand the vagaries of the weather. Such benefits improve the quality of the end product.

Kunekune

Characteristics

Weight: male/female
140–200 lb (63.5–91 kg).

Color: varies between
ginger, brown, black,
cream, and spotted.
Usually has a pair of
tassels under the chin
named "piri piri."

Kunekune (pronounced "kooneykooney") is Maori for "fat and round." The pig breed of the same name—and also known as the Maori Pig—is a delightful-looking little pig with stout legs and a short, round body. It is placid, easy to keep, and enjoys human company. It feeds mainly on grass, so is a good lawn mower.

Although the breed is from New Zealand, its true country of origin remains in doubt. It is possible the Maoris introduced it to the island, as similar breeds can be found in Polynesia. Whalers from various countries released pigs on the islands as a food supply for later visits. Pigs that were left by Captain Cook on his first voyage to the island may also have contributed to the Kunekune. Zoe Lindop and Andrew Calveley brought the Kunekune to Britain in 1992.

Large Black

Characteristics

Weight: male
700–800 lb
(320–360 kg); female
600–700 lb (270–320 kg)

Color: black

The Large Black is Britain's only all-black pig. It originates from the Old English hog of the sixteenth and seventeenth centuries. In the late nineteenth century, there were two types of Large Black: one in Devon and Cornwall and the other in East Anglia. The Large Black Society brought them together in 1889. This breed is found throughout the country and kept in small herds, some of which were established in the early twentieth century.

In the 1960s, a trend toward intensive rearing led to a decline in the breed, since it was unsuitable for this type of farming. Extremely docile and hardy, it is ideally suited to simple outdoor rearing systems. This characteristic, and its color, made it popular for overseas breeding and, by 1935, it had been exported to more than thirty countries.

Large Black sows are excellent mothers, able to bring up large litters on basic food. These animals once grazed orchards, eating windfall, and would be fed whey, a by-product of butter production. The Large Black produces meat of superb quality.

Large White (Yorkshire)

Characteristics

Weight: male
772–838 lb
(350–380 kg); female
573–661 lb
(260–300 kg)

Color: white hair and
pink skin. Slightly dished
face and erect ears.

The history of the Large White is difficult to trace. Its origins go back to its native Yorkshire in the north of England. It first came to prominence at the Royal Windsor Show in 1831 and was registered as a breed in 1884. It is believed the breed was the result of a cross between the Cumberland, Leicestershire, Middle White, and Small White, plus Chinese and Siamese pigs that were owned by John Tulley of Keighley in West Yorkshire, England. The Small White became extinct in 1912, and the last Cumberland died in Cumbria in 1960.

The Large White was developed to be almost self-sufficient and is happy spending its life foraging outdoors. It is hardy and can withstand varying and extreme climates as well as producing large litters. By the end of the nineteenth century, the Large White was well established worldwide and is said to be the world's most popular breed of pig. In the United States and Canada, it is known as the Yorkshire. It produces top-quality meat under any name.

Mangalitza

Characteristics

Weight: male
150–179 lb
(68–77 kg); female
141–161 lb (64–73 kg)

Color: blonde, swallow-bellied (white lower body, black upper), and red (ginger).

This is an ancient breed with curly wool. Native to Hungary and Austria, it is now found throughout the British Isles, the United States, Canada, and Europe. In the early years of the twentieth century, it was crossed with a Lincolnshire Curly Coat, the result of which was exported to Hungary and Austria. The Lincolnshire Curly Coat became extinct in 1972.

Mangalitza meat products were, at one time, in great demand all over Europe and were even traded on the Vienna Stock Exchange. The breed was famed for its hardiness, in part due to the curly coat that provides superb insulation. It is able to survive the harshest winters and long, hot summers without the problem of sunburn. In 2006, Tony York of Pig Paradise Farm in the UK imported three males, one of each color, and fourteen females, with hopes to establish herds of this excellent breed in the British Isles. Traditionally, the meat is used for salami and prosciutto because of its superb flavor.

Meidam

Characteristics

Weight: male
500–700 lb
(226–318 kg); female
450–600 lb
(204–272 kg)

Color: white with pink
skin. Semi-lop ears.

The Meidam (pronounced "maydam") is a modern breed native to the British Isles, accepted and registered as a breed at the beginning of the twenty-first century. Its genetic makeup is approximately a quarter Meishan, a quarter Large White, and half Landrace. The aim is to capture the advantages of the Meishan, which include larger litter sizes and excellent mothering ability. At the same time, the breed retains the European breed's benefits of growth and excellent lean meat. So, this is a "synthetic" breed, created with a commercial purpose, but using the genes of long-established pure breeds. This is not the first time Chinese pig genes have been used to establish a "native" British breed. It is thought that, in the 1800s, an importation of Chinese pigs was interbred with pigs that eventually contributed to the Large White breed.

Meishan

Characteristics

Weight: male/female
140 lb (62 kg)

Color: black. Heavily
wrinkled face and skin;
lop ears cover their eyes.

Found in most countries, the Meishan (pronounced "mayshawn") originates from a narrow belt of land between north and central China in the lower Changjiang River basin—an area of lakes and valleys with a mild climate. The pigs are well fed on farm by-products, water, plants, and concentrates. The Meishan is fat and slow growing but has excellent-tasting meat. When the breed was first imported to the British Isles in the 1980s, upon seeing two Meishan lying down, one man remarked, "It's like looking at a pile of old coats." The breed is relatively disease resistant, docile, and an extremely good mother. In the UK, it is usually crossed with the Large White to produce top-quality meat: the best of Yorkshire and China brought together for a superb result.

Ossabaw Island Hog

Characteristics

Weight: male/female
200 lb (90 kg)

Color: black or black and spotted. Heavy coat, long nose, and pricked up ears.

These hogs are native to Ossabaw Island, Georgia, in the United States, and a few are still found there and elsewhere in Georgia. They are the descendants of animals brought to this New World island more than 450 years ago.

The Ossabaw Island hog is a small breed, being less than 20 inches (51 centimeters) tall, and extremely rare. In most environments, feral pigs will cross with the domestic breeds, but this was not the case on Ossabaw Island. These pigs have developed and bred in total isolation. Food is scarce in spring. Over the centuries the breed has adapted to the food cycle with a method of storing fat to see it through periods of short supply. Over the years, the breed has also become smaller. Today, quarantine restrictions prevent exporting the hogs directly from the island—the herds on the mainland descend from a group that left the island in 1970, prior to these restrictions. The meat is of superb quality with a fat profile high in omega-3. It is beautifully marbled and has a rich, wild flavor.

Oxford Sandy and Black

Characteristics

Weight: 550–660 lb
(250–300 kg)

Color: pale to dark gold
with black blotches,
not spots; the boar has
a white tip to the tail,
four white feet, and
a white blaze (stripe
down the center of the
face). Ears are lopped or
semi-lopped.

The Oxford Sandy and Black is native to Oxfordshire, England, where it was a traditional cottager's pig and has been in existence for more than 300 years. It is also one of the oldest pig breeds in the British Isles. The main body color is due to its Tamworth ancestry.

The breed was in decline in the 1940s, and by 1985, extinction seemed inevitable. Were it not for the efforts and dedication of three men, the Oxford Sandy and Black would be no more.

The Oxford Sandy and Black is also known as the Plum Porridge, the Plum Pudding, and the Oxford Forest. The breed is happiest outdoors in woodland and rough grazing. Its color gives it a greater protection against sunburn. The Oxford Sandy and Black is docile and easy to manage, ideal for smallholders, and produces meat of excellent quality and flavor.

Pietrain

Characteristics

Weight: male
530–570 lb
(240–260 kg), female
485–530 lb (220–240 kg)

Color: white with
black spots; the spots
surrounded with rings
of light pigmentation
that carries white hair,
giving it a piebald look.
Erect ears.

The Pietrain is named for the town in Belgium where it was bred in 1940. It is a cross between a local white Landrace-type pig and the French Bayeux, which is a descendent of the Berkshire. The breeding was small scale until after the Second World War, when the Pietrain began to be noted for its quality meat. In 1964, the UK's Pig Industry Development Board (PIDB) imported eighty-four pigs. Six boars and a number of gilts (young females) were kept by the PIDB for crossbreeding experiments. The remainder were distributed to the Animal Breeding and Research Organization in Edinburgh, Wye College in Kent, and T. Wall and Sons. These would mainly be used to improve existing breeds.

The Royal Welsh Festival has pig agility races through cones and hoops just for fun. They are frequently won by happy and healthy Pietrains. The breed's low-fat meat regularly wins national gold and silver medals for its quality.

Poland China

Characteristics

Weight: male
550–800 lb
(250–363 kg); female
500–650 lb (226–295 kg)

Color: usually black with
six white patches.

This breed, originally native to Miami Valley, Butler, and Warren Counties, Ohio, is found throughout the United States and Cyprus. It owes its origins to so many different breeds of pig it is difficult to know where to start. In 1816, John Wallace bought four Big China hogs—one boar and three sows. Two of the sows were white and the third had black spots. These Big China hogs were popular in Virginia, Maryland, Pennsylvania, and Kentucky. There is also evidence pointing to the bloodline of pigs bred by the Duke of Bedford, which have similar coloring and came from Kentucky around this time.

Whatever its origins, the quality of its meat is superb. There are two important requirements when breeding the Poland China: it has to be large and it has to be able to travel. The pigs were driven to market, and this frequently meant a journey of 100 miles. If you are in the United States or Cyprus, look out for the Poland China: it is magnificent.

Tamworth

Characteristics

Weight: male
550–820 lb
(230–370 kg); female
440–660 lb
(200–300 kg)

Color: a rich, golden-
brown. Pricked up ears.

This breed originated on Sir Robert Peel's estate at Tamworth in
Staffordshire, England, in the early nineteenth century, and is classed as
one of the purest English native breeds. It is considered a little on the
primitive side because of its long snout (the longest of any modern breed)
and pricked ears. Its beautiful color is credited to the introduction of a
red boar from Ireland. The breed was imported into the United States in
1882 by Thomas Bennett of Illinois and soon after into Canada where,
from 1913 to mid-century, it reached peak numbers accounting for 10
percent of the total swine population. It was also exported to Australia
and Southeast Asia. Records from this time show feral pigs similar to the
Tamworth running around the Otago region in New Zealand.

The Tamworth is ideal for rearing in outdoor systems and is good
for reclaiming wood and scrub land—the perfect four-legged plowing
machine. In winter, it lives quite happily in well-built huts in a snow-
covered field. Its golden-brown color gives protection from sunburn.
Although now rare, the Tamworth is still bred for its excellent meat.

Vietnamese Pot-Bellied

Characteristics

Weight: male 110 lb
(50 kg); female 106 lb
(48 kg)

Color: black. Short legs,
short straight tail, small
upright ears, and a low-
hanging belly.

Native to the Red River Delta in Vietnam, this breed is now found in the British Isles, United States, Canada, Europe, the Middle East, Indonesia, and Japan. It has been crossed with so many breeds it is impossible to find a purebred. There are approximately 2.5 million Vietnamese Pot-Bellies in their native country.

The breed arrived in Europe and the United States in the 1960s and was popular with zoos and animal parks in the 1970s. Ten years on, the idea of keeping a pig as a pet took off. In the United States, in 1986, a Vietnamese Pot-Bellied cost several thousand dollars. The original breed was far from ideal as a household pet, but improvements have been made since then. It is now a great pet for those with a large garden or smallholding, and it has an extremely good temperament.

Welsh

Characteristics

Weight: male/female
271–304 lb (123–138 kg)

Color: white. Pear-shaped when viewed from above or the side; lop ears meet just short of the snout.

Raised in Wales long before living memory, this breed came to prominence in 1870, when large numbers were sold into Cheshire, England, for fattening on milk by-products. The Welsh Pig Society in West Wales was founded in 1920. The Old Glamorgan Pig Society (established 1918) represented breeds similar to the Welsh from various areas of Wales. In 1922, the two societies amalgamated and became the Welsh Pig Society.

The Welsh reached its peak in popularity in 1947. In 1955, the scientist Dr. J. Hammond advised the government that the Welsh pig was one of the three breeds on which the British pig industry should be founded, the other two being the Large White and the Landrace. The breed began to gain attention outside its home area, in the eastern counties of England, the Midlands, and Yorkshire—areas that were dominated by the Large White and the British Landrace—because of its hardy breed traits with the ability to survive under most indoor or outdoor conditions. The breed is now at risk.

Wild Boar

Characteristics

Weight: male
165–220 lb
(75–100 kg); female
130–180 lb (60–80 kg)

Color: a thick, bristly
brown, reddish-brown,
black, or dark gray coat.
Male has upper and
lower tusks, the female
has only lower.

The wild boar is the ancestor of the modern-day domestic pig. It became extinct in the British Isles for the first time in the early fourteenth century, but was reintroduced by King James I and his son, who brought them to the New Forest from Germany. The animals left a path of devastation wherever they appeared and were not popular with the local residents. During the seventeenth century, Britain once more became a wild-boar-free zone. It was almost 300 years before the breed reappeared on British farms. Some were released from captivity, either by accident or design, and there are now several "sounders" (groups of feral wild boars) roaming the British countryside. Young borelets have brown-and-white stripes, which provide excellent camouflage when hiding in undergrowth. The meat is red to rose colored and apparently tastes like "best beef with crackling."

SHEEP

Sheep have provided people with food, drink, and clothing for more than 10,000 years. When first domesticated in Mesopotamia (modern-day Iraq, Turkey, and Iran), these wild Mouflon sheep were much smaller than modern domestic breeds and covered in coarse, colored wool. The sheep slowly moved west into Western Europe and then on to the Americas (both North and South). Softer, whiter fleeces typically are more desirable and profitable. Many of the very early writers describe the process of selective breeding, which continues to this day to provide the consumer (and the sheep) with the best of everything.

Many cities in the British Isles and throughout Europe were built on the wealth that quality wool provided. Bradford in the north of England was once the center of the international wool trade with its magnificent Yorkshire stone Wool Exchange, where deals worth millions of pounds were agreed and sealed with a shake of the hand. How things change!

A number of the ancient breeds are at risk of extinction, and were it not for the dedication of small breeders would disappear altogether. Typically, they are not commercially viable and are bred for the pleasure they give and specialty markets such as hand-felting and rug-weaving. The rare breeds and the upland sheep keep many of the inaccessible areas of our countryside under control, through conservation grazing.

Beulah Speckled Face

Characteristics

Weight: ram 190 lb (86 kg), ewe 115 lb (52 kg)

Fleece weight: 1¾–5¾ lb (1.75–2.5 kg)

The breed is naturally polled (without horns).

This breed (full name Eppynt Hill Beulah Speckled Face) is most usually seen in its homeland of Wales, although it can be found elsewhere in the British Isles and Europe. The true origins of the breed are unknown, but these sheep have been grazing the hills of Wales for several hundred years and have adapted to the local environment. This is a hardy sheep, grazing on grasses and herbs at an altitude of 1,000–1,500 feet (305–450 meters), and is also in demand for conservation grazing.

The quality wool is used for tweed, fine flannel, hand-spinning, weaving, and knitting. The coarser wool is used in rug- and carpet-making. The Beulah Speckled Face also produces quality lean meat. The breed is not known to be timid, and tends to ignore dogs, but if young lambs are present the ewe will attack the dog.

Black Welsh Mountain

Characteristics

Weight: ram 143 lb (65 kg), ewe 100 lb (45 kg)

Fleece weight: 2½–5½ lb (1–2.5 kg)

The rams have impressive horns that curve around the ears, and the ewes are polled.

This is an ancient breed that was recorded in the Middle Ages when it was prized for its quality meat as well as its wool. It is the only black sheep breed in the UK, with the tips of the fleece bleaching to a reddish brown in the sun. Around 200 years ago in the mountain flock, an occasional black lamb was born; from that time some shepherds decided to breed only black sheep, improving the fleece and the meat quality at the same time. The Black Welsh Mountain was recognized as a breed in 1922, and was exported to the United States in 1972.

This hardy, disease-resistant breed is quite able to take care of itself in its harsh living environment. The wool can be used in its natural color or mixed with other fibers. It is used undyed for fine tweed; the wool produces a durable, light, and warm cloth. The meat is also of excellent quality with a distinct flavor.

Blackface

Characteristics

Weight: ram 150–170 lb
(68–77 kg), ewe 115–
130 lb (52–59 kg)

Fleece weight: 3¼–7 lb
(1.7–3 kg)

The rams and ewes are
both horned.

The history of the Blackface (or Scottish Blackface) is lost in the mists of time. Monks in the twelfth century bred sheep that are the ancestors of the Blackface. They used the wool to make clothing and exported wool to Europe. In 1503, it is recorded that James IV of Scotland had a flock of around 5,000 strong and improved the breed. During the Highland Clearances in Scotland in the mid-eighteenth to mid-nineteenth centuries, tenant farmers were removed, sometimes forcibly, to make way for the Blackface. It has developed over many years, surviving in a harsh climate and not always having the finest grazing.

Today it is found in the Scottish Highlands, the Scottish Borders, the Pennines, Dartmoor, and Northern Ireland, as well as the United States, Argentina, and Italy. The long, coarse wool is a protection against the harsh weather in their chosen grazing ground.

The first-quality wool is used to produce the world-famous Harris Tweed, the medium class is used in the manufacture of quality carpets around the world, and the remainder is exported to Italy to be used as mattress filling. In the United States, it is used for rugs and horse blankets. The breed is also known for its top-quality meat.

Blueface Leicester

Characteristics

Weight: ram 240 lb (110 kg), ewe 196 lb (89 kg)

Fleece weight: 2½–4½ lb (1–2 kg)

The rams and ewes are polled.

The breed was developed in the UK in the 1700s by Robert Bakewell and originally called the Dishley Leicester, becoming the Bluefaced Leicester in the early twentieth century. The fleece is usually white but can be brown ("moorit"); the skin on the head is blue, and it has a handsome Roman nose. It is not a hardy breed, a trait common in most fine-wool breeds. The prime purpose of this highly commercial breed is to cross-breed with hardy hill ewes—Blackface, Swaledale, Welsh Mountain, and Cheviot—to produce Mule ewes. Mule, in this context, means any cross-bred sired by a Bluefaced Leicester. Mules make up over 50 percent of cross-bred ewes.

The Bluefaced Leicester is mainly used for meat but the fleece—which is tightly purled, like tiny knots—is used in the making of quality cloth and is becoming increasingly popular for hand-spinning and knitting wool. A record $30,000 (around £23,000 guineas) has been paid for a brown ram. Exported to Canada in 1970, the breed then found its way to the United States, and is also found in New Zealand and Australia.

Border Leicester

Characteristics

Weight: ram 308–386 lb
(140–175 kg), ewe 198–
264 lb (90–120 kg)

Fleece weight: 13–19 lb
(6–9 kg)

The rams and ewes
are polled.

The Border Leicester is a large, long breed with a Roman nose. It can be found all over the British Isles, and is a descendant of the Dishley Leicester (see Bluefaced Leicester).

Robert Bakewell was a disciple of the English agricultural pioneers Jethro Tull and Viscount Townshend (known to his friends as "Turnip"). Prior to the innovative work of such people in the eighteenth century, all sheep were allowed to breed as and when they liked. Bakewell separated the breeds and allowed mating only at specific times, between "matching" ewes and rams. These changes drastically improved the breed, which was developed in the border country of Northumberland; as a result, in 1850 this New Leicester became the Border Leicester. Whether it was the Teeswater or the Cheviot that was used to create the breed is a much-debated point.

This popular breed is now found in Australia, New Zealand, South Africa, France, Spain, Portugal, Canada, the United States, and many other countries. The excellent-quality, long, lustrous wool is used by hand-spinners and as knitting wool; the meat is of good quality.

Clun Forest

Characteristics

Weight: ram 175–200 lb (79–91 kg), ewe 130–160 lb (59–72 kg)

Fleece weight: 4½–5¾ lb (2–2.5 kg)

The rams and ewes are without horns.

The hardy Clun Forest breed originated in the area surrounding the Clun Forest in Shropshire, England, in the early 1800s, and the Clun Forest Sheep Breeders Society was formed 100 years later. It is believed seminomadic shepherds living in the forest 1,000 years ago were the original breeders, and the sheep can still be found grazing the hills around the Welsh Borders. Apart from meat and wool, the Clun Forest is also bred for its superb milk that is high in butterfat, as a result of which the lambs, usually twins, grow quickly. It is crossed with dairy breeds of sheep to improve the quality of sheep cheeses.

The breed is also found in the United States, mainly in Virginia, and in France, the Netherlands, and the Czech Republic. The breed is known for its quality meat and creamy white fleece, which is used in hosiery and knitting yarns. Large quantities are exported to Japan for use in futons.

Dalesbred

Characteristics

Weight: ram 121–165 lb (55–75 kg), ewe 99–132 lb (4–60 kg)

Fleece weight: 3½–5½ lb (1.5–2.5 kg)

The rams and ewes are both horned.

A tough northern sheep, the Dalesbred is bred for a purpose and to suit the area in which it lives. In 1930, the local breeders got together to "fix" the type of sheep they had been breeding for hundreds of years. This hardy breed is very adaptable to climatic change, and with its thick white fleece can survive the bleakest of conditions on the bleak moors of the central Pennines and the hills of Cumbria, England. The Dalesbred does not need to be fenced in; the sheep happily stay in their own area. This natural instinct, passed from ewe to lamb over succeeding generations and common to all sheep living in large areas of common land, is known as hefting.

The Dalesbred has a distinctive white mark on each side of the nose, and is one of the maternal parents of the Masham and Mule sheep that are the mainstay of lowland farming. It produces quality meat and the wool is used for tweed and carpets.

Derbyshire Gritstone

Characteristics

The rams and ewes are without horns.

Weight: ram 176–220 lb (80–100 kg), ewe 121–143 lb (55–65 kg)

Fleece weight: 4½–7 lb (2–3 kg)

The rams and ewes are both horned.

This breed is found in the Peak District of Derbyshire and the Pennine District of Yorkshire and Lancashire in England, as well as in Scotland, the Outer Hebrides, and Wales. The Derbyshire Gritstone is one of the oldest British breeds, originating in what was the Dale of Goyt (now the Goyt Valley) in the Derbyshire Peak District in the mid-eighteenth century, but sheep have been bred in this area since the Middle Ages. The Derbyshire Gritstone was originally called the Dale O'Goyt sheep. It is a hardy, good-looking, adaptable, disease-resistant breed, well able to survive the harsh conditions up to 2,000 feet (650 meters) above sea level. Due to the high quality of the ewes' milk, the lambs grow quickly.

The fleeces have won many prizes, including the prestigious Overall Champion fleece at the Great Yorkshire Show. The wool is one of the finest hosiery wools available in the British Isles, and is also used for knitted outerwear and underwear. The coarser wool is used for carpets. The Derbyshire Gritstone produces the finest-quality meat.

Devon and Cornwall Longwool

Characteristics

The rams and ewes are without horns.

Weight: ram 220–242 lb (100–110 kg), ewe 165–176 lb (75–80 kg)

Fleece weight: 15–22 lb (7–10 kg)

The rams and ewes are both horned.

The Devon and Cornwall Longwool is seldom found outside the southwest of the British Isles, and the origins of the breed can be traced back to the seventeenth century. This large and sturdy grassland breed developed from two of the oldest West Country breeds—the South Devon and the Devon Longwool—and produces one of the heaviest fleeces in Great Britain.

The Devon and Cornwall produces so much wool that the lambs can be sheared, the wool being highly prized for knitwear, flannels, and dress fabrics. The creamy white fleece may not be beautiful, but it is very strong and hard-wearing and can be used for tweed, but mainly for carpets and rugs. The Devon and Cornwall Longwool also produces quality meat.

Devon Closewool

Characteristics

Weight: ram 198–220 lb
(90–100 kg), ewe 132–
136 lb (60–62 kg)

Fleece weight: 6–7 lb
(2.5–3.5 kg)

Rams and ewes
are polled.

The Devon Closewool was found originally in and around Exmoor (North Devon and Somerset), England, but can now be seen throughout Devon and Cornwall, Somerset, and parts of Wales. This hardy grassland breed has existed for over a hundred years, and originates from crossing the Exmoor Horn and Devon Longwool. The dense white fleece gives excellent protection from the driving wind and rain coming off the Atlantic Ocean onto Exmoor and North Devon. The breed can survive and flourish in these extreme conditions with little or no help, whereas many other breeds would perish; the dense fleece prevents the rain from reaching the skin. The rams are used with other breeds to improve the latter's hardiness and quality.

In 2015, a small company was set up to experiment in producing cheese from the quality milk. The superb wool is used to enhance the rugged appearance of many tweeds and is also used for hosiery fabrics and carpets. The Devon Closewool produces quality meat.

Dorset Down

Characteristics

Weight: ram 242 lb (110 kg), ewe 154 lb (70 kg)

Fleece weight: 5 lb (2.25 kg)

The rams and ewes are without horns.

In the early 1800s in England, Homer Saunders of Watercombe and Humphrey of Chaddleworth created a much-improved local Down breed by crossing local Wiltshire, Hampshire, and Berkshire ewes with a Southdown ram, and the breed thrived. The fleece is white; the face, ears, and legs are brown. This powerful, stocky breed can now be seen mainly in southern England, the West Midlands, and Wales; flocks can also be found in Europe, New Zealand, Australia, the United States, and South America. Although it is not found in large numbers, it is an adaptable and easily handled breed, capable of producing fast-rowing lambs on grass alone.

The white fleece is short and fine, and the wool of the Dorset Down is classed by the British Wool Marketing Board as one of the best in the country. This quality wool is blended with other wools to improve quality. It is also used for flannel and dress material and specialty knitting yarns, but especially for futons in Japan. The Dorset Down produces delicately flavored meat.

Dorset Horn and Polled Dorset

Characteristics

Weight: ram 225–275 lb (102–125 kg), ewe 150–200 lb (68–91 kg)

Fleece weight: 5–6½ lb (2.25–3 kg)

In the horned variety, the ram's horns are heavy and spiralled; the ewe's horns are light with a gentle forward curve.

The Dorset is an ancient breed that is believed to have developed from whitefaced, horned, short-woolled sheep that lived in the hill pastures of southwestern England and has probably been around since the seventeenth century. The Polled Dorset was developed in Australia in the 1900s; American breeders produced their own Polled Dorset in the 1950s. Most sheep are seasonal breeders, mating in autumn for spring lambs, but the Dorset has the rare ability to breed the year round.

The white fleece produces one of the highest-quality white wools known in the UK and is used for dress fabrics, flannel, hosiery, fine tweed, and specialty knitting yarns, and for lining boots. The Dorset Horn also produces quality meat.

The Polled Dorset is identical apart from the fact that the breed has no horns.

Est à Laine Merino

Characteristics

Weight: ram 265–287 lb (120–30 kg), ewe 154–187 lb (70–85 kg).

Fleece weight: 11–16¾ lb (5–7.5 kg).

Both rams and ewes are naturally polled.

The Est à Laine Merino originated in France and Spain but is now found throughout the British Isles, Europe, and most other continents. The original Merino was developed by an indigenous North African people who were, in 1340, defeated by the Spaniards. As a result, sheep fell into the hands of Spanish royalty and finally arrived in France. Over 200 years ago, sheep grazing in the Alsace Lorraine region of France were improved using the Merino. These sheep became known as the Est à Laine Merino, bred essentially for the quality of the wool, which is now frequently compared to cashmere.

The breed arrived in the British Isles in 1978. This hardy yet docile animal has the ability to survive on poor grazing and cope with the British weather. The fine-quality wool is used for superb-quality knitwear; the Est à Laine Merino also produces quality meat.

Exmoor Horn

Characteristics

Weight: ram 160 lb (73 kg), ewe 110 lb (50 kg)

Fleece weight: 7–14 lb (3–6 kg)

The rams and ewes have large curling horns.

The Exmoor Horn has white fleece and black nostrils and cherry-colored skin. It is a direct descendant of the ancient breed that has existed since time immemorial and has genetically developed to live on the open hilly moorland of Exmoor in the English West Country. This hill breed is able to survive the harsh winters on Exmoor and the bleak Brendon Hills up to 1,500 feet (450 meters) above sea level, on grass alone, and still produce sufficient milk to feed the lambs.

It is also one of the very few hill breeds that produces fine-quality wool. The Exmoor Horn was a major influence on the West Country's reputation for quality wool. The area is famous for special wool cloths of superb quality and finish; other uses are for hosiery, felts, knitting yarns, and quality tweed. It has been said that "its irascible, defiant grumpiness has ensured its survival—this is wool with attitude." The Exmoor Horn also produces quality meat.

Greyface Dartmoor

Characteristics

Weight: ram 165–220 lb
(75–100 kg), ewe 132–
154 lb (60–70 kg)

Fleece weight: 12–17 lb
(5.5–8 kg), but can be as
high as 33 lb (15 kg)

The rams and ewes are
without horns.

The Greyface Dartmoor, also called the Dartmoor or the improved Dartmoor, has been in existence for over a century, descended, developed, and improved by crossing with other local breeds during the seventeenth and eighteenth centuries. Many believe the Greyface was descended from the Iron Age Soay sheep. There is ample evidence that wool has been produced in and around Dartmoor since the thirteenth century; Richard I gave the monks of Buckfast Abbey permission to graze their sheep in 1190. Today they can be found throughout England, Wales, and southern Scotland.

The Dartmoor, with its creamy white fleece (the woolly head and legs give it the appearance of an Old English Sheepdog), has a superb constitution enabling it to survive the harshest of winters. The wool is used for blankets, carpets, and wool cloths. The Dartmoor also produces top-quality meat.

Hampshire Down

Characteristics

Weight: ram 265 lb (120 kg), ewe 200 lb (91 kg)

Fleece weight: 6–10 lb (2.7–4.5 kg)

The rams and ewes are without horns.

The Hampshire Down was established over 150 years ago and was developed from the Berkshire Knot (now extinct), Old Hampshire, Southdown, and Wiltshire Horn. The lambs are noted for being robust and hardy. Another economic advantage is the breed's speed of growth when compared to others, and its ability to survive the extremes of a British winter and the heat of a continental summer without shelter.

The Hampshire Down is now found in over forty countries. Those exported to the United States in the 1860s were almost wiped out by the Civil War, and imports did not start again until twenty years later. The fine and dense wool is used for hand-knitting, hosiery, felts and flannels, and futons in Japan. The Hampshire Down also produces top-quality meat.

Herdwick

Characteristics

Weight: ram 145–165 (66–75 kg), ewe 77–99 lb (35–45 kg)

Fleece weight: 3–4½ lb (1.5–2 kg)

The rams have creamy white curved horns; the ewes are without horns.

The Herdwick is an ancient breed found mainly in the Lake District in the British Isles and is uniquely adapted to its wild environment in the high, unfenced fells of Cumbria that exceed 3,000 feet (305 meters). The Herdwick lives its entire life in the mountains with little supplementary feeding. The lambs are born black and change color over two years, learning from their mothers where to graze and shelter on the fells. This strong homing instinct means the sheep stay in family groups, helping the shepherds manage their flocks. Their grazing has helped to shape the landscape of the beautiful Lake District, now recognized as a UNESCO World Heritage Site.

The famous children's author Beatrix Potter kept Herdwick sheep and bought Herdwick farms, which she gifted to the National Trust on her death in 1943 to conserve the unique farming practices of the Lake District. The coarse wool from the gray-blue fleece is used for carpets, specialty fabrics, and knitting wools. The Herdwick also produces top-quality meat.

Hill Radnor

Characteristics

Weight: ram 154–176 lb (70–80 kg), ewe 77–121 lb (50–55 kg)

Fleece weight: 3½–4½ lb (1.5–2 kg)

The rams have long curved horns spiraling outward; the ewes are without horns.

The Hill Radnor is a native mountain hill breed with a thick, creamy white fleece and a tan face. It was developed in Radnorshire in Wales in a period beyond living memory. It is a hardy, healthy breed and can survive in both lowland and mountain environments, in the worst weather conditions, and on limited and frequently poor-quality forage. It is also resistant to many of the contagious sheep diseases. The Hill Radnor, like many other breeds, suffered severely during the foot-and-mouth epidemic of 2001. This breed can be found in Powys and Gwent and surrounding areas.

The wool is used for high-quality fabrics such as fine tweed and soft flannel, and is in great demand by local hand-spinners and weavers. The Hill Radnor also produces top-quality meat.

Hog Island

Characteristics

Weight: ram 125 lb (57 kg), ewe 90 lb (41 kg)

Fleece weight: 2–8 lb (1–3.5 kg)

About half the rams and ewes have horns.

The Hog Island is a feral breed from Hog Island, Virginia, which was colonized in the seventeenth century. The breed would have originated from British breeds—possibly the Improved Leicester crossbred, now called the Leicester Longwool—and the Merino that grazed the barrier islands, with a mixture of Spanish breeds that escaped from ships wrecked locally. They were bred mainly for wool and food. A hurricane destroyed the island in 1933; it was abandoned by the inhabitants, and the sheep were left to fend for themselves. In 1974, the island was bought by the Nature Conservancy, and the sheep were removed and settled in various locations, including George Washington's birthplace, Mount Vernon, and Colonial Williamsburg, a living history museum in Virginia.

The fleeces are mainly white and about 10 percent are black; the lambs are born spotted or speckled. The wool is in demand for hand-knitting, and the meat is good.

Jacob

Characteristics

Weight: ram 120–180 lb (265–397 kg) ewe 80–120 lb (176–265 kg)

Fleece weight: 3–6 lb (1.75–2.75 kg)

The rams and ewes have two to six horns.

The origins of the Jacob, also known as the Spanish sheep, are unclear (one of the earliest records of the breed being selectively bred can be found in the Bible: Genesis, chapter 30). The breed's color and markings are thought to have originated in Syria 3,000 years ago. From there the Jacob moved through the Iberian Peninsula, arriving on the UK's shores almost 400 years ago. Another theory is that they were brought to the UK by the Vikings. In the Middle Ages, they were kept for ornamental purposes, grazing parkland. The oldest known flock, which was imported in the 1750s, is at Charlecote Park in Warwickshire, England.

The Jacob is a healthy, easily managed breed. The most common color for the fleece is white with black patches, and the wool has a niche market for people wishing to use naturally colored wool. It is in great demand by hand-spinners and was also used in clothing exported to the United States from Britain in the 1950s and 1960s. It also produces quality meat.

Katahdin

Characteristics

Weight: ram 180–250 lb (82–113 kg), ewe 120–160 lb (54.5–72.5 kg)

No fleece.

The rams can have horns; the ewes are polled.

The Katahdin was developed in Maine, United States, in the mid-twentieth century, and is a cross between the St. Croix breed and mainly the Suffolk from the UK. The St. Croix is named after its home island in the Caribbean and was imported into the United States by Michael Piel. The coat—which can be any color—is hair, not wool, and consists of a coarse overcoat and a woolly fiber undercoat. The thickness of the coat depends on the severity of the weather. Come the warmer weather, the sheep sheds the coat naturally.

This breed has become increasingly popular as the price of wool falls, since the cost of shearing a sheep can exceed the value of the fleece. The Katahdin are excellent mothers, and the lambs, usually twins, are vigorous and alert from birth. Triplets and quads are not unknown. The meat is excellent.

Kerry Hill

Characteristics

Weight: ram 143–154 lb
(65–70 kg), ewe 121–
143 lb (55–65 kg)

Fleece weight: 4½–7 lb
(2–3 kg)

The rams and ewes
are without horns.

No wool on
head and legs.

The breed originated in and is named after the village of Kerry on the Welsh–English border. The earliest mention of the breed was in 1809, and it can now be found throughout Great Britain, Ireland, the Netherlands, Germany, and Denmark. The Kerry Hill is easily recognizable, with distinctive black-and-white markings. The ewes are excellent mothers and are just as happy on the lowlands as on the uplands.

In the twentieth century, numbers rapidly declined and the breed was put on the "At Risk" register, but by 2006 the numbers had greatly improved and it was out of danger. The wool, from the creamy white fleece, is among the softest in Great Britain and is used for tweed, flannel, knitwear, and furnishing fabrics, being especially suitable for deep-textured designs. The Kerry Hill also produces top-quality meat.

Leicester Longwool

Characteristics

The rams and ewes are without horns.

Weight: ram 200–300 lb (91–136 kg), ewe 150–200 lb (68–91 kg)

Fleece weight: 11–18 lb (5–8 kg)

Today's Leicester Longwool is a direct descendant of a breed developed from the old Leicester sheep in the 1700s by Robert Bakewell. The breed has an interesting history and has been known by various names, including the Bakewell Leicester and the English Leicester. This is a large, tough, hardy sheep, capable of surviving the rigors of the British climate; it does not, however, like standing around in the rain for too long. Rattle a feed bucket and they will come running.

From its humble beginnings it can now be found in many parts of the UK, but mainly in the northeast. It is also found in Australia, the United States, and New Zealand. The fleece is a curly, creamy white, and the wool is used for suit linings, knitting, rug-making, hand-spinning, tapestry, wall hangings, and soft furnishings. The Leicester Longwool also produces quality meat.

Lincoln Longwool

Characteristics

The rams and ewes are without horns.

Weight: ram 265–353 lb (120–160 kg), ewe 176–265 lb (80–120 kg)

Fleece weight: 11–20 lb (5.5–9 kg)

The Lincoln Longwool is the largest of the longwool sheep and has been developed and improved over many hundreds of years; a breed with a curly fleece of the Lincoln type was first mentioned in the 1300s. The breed as we know it today has developed from its ancestors in the Middle Ages; in the 1700s, Robert Bakewell used it as a foundation stock for his work. A society to safeguard the breed was formed in 1796. The first improvements were to produce hard-wearing, strong, lustrous wool. Over time further developments were carried out to turn it into a dual-purpose breed, with a woolly forelock.

In the British Isles it is found mainly in Lincolnshire, but it is also dotted around the country. It is also found in the United States, Australia, and New Zealand. The wool is used for quality suiting, upholstery, carpets, dolls' wigs, plush soft toys, hand-spinning, and weaving. The Lincoln Longwool also produces top-quality meat.

Llanwenog

Characteristics

The rams and ewes are without horns. There is a tuft of crew-cut wool on the forehead.

Weight: ram 176–199 lb (80–90 kg), ewe 121–132 lb (55–60 kg)

Fleece weight: 4½–5¾ lb (2–2.5 kg)

The Llanwenog (pronounced "thlanwenog") can trace its origins to the late 1800s in west Wales. It was developed from a cross of the now extinct Llanllwni (a black-faced horned breed) and Shropshire sheep that had recently arrived in the area. The result was a polled black-faced breed: the Llanwenog had arrived. This cross produced the best of both worlds: the wool and meat from the ram and the quality milk and toughness of the Llanllwni ewe.

This breed will thrive in harsh conditions 1,000 feet (305 meters) above sea level, but can also take advantage of the lowland pastures. The Llanwenog is easier to shepherd than most Welsh sheep, having little desire to wander. They live longer than many other breeds and produce many lambs. The creamy white fleece produces wool that is very soft to the touch and is prized by hand-spinners and is used for fine tweed, hosiery, flannel, and knitting wool. The Llanwenog also produces top-quality meat.

Lleyn

Characteristics

The rams and ewes are without horns.

Weight: ram 165–107 lb (75–85 kg), ewe 143–154 lb (65–70 kg)

Fleece weight: 6–8 lb (2.5–3.5 kg)

The Lleyn (pronounced "kleen") sheep, named after the Lleyn Peninsula in North Wales, can trace its roots to Ireland in the 1750s when Robert Bakewell took some of his Dishley Leicesters to Ireland to cross-breed them with local stock and so created the Roscommon breed. The Roscommon arrived on the Lleyn Peninsula in the early 1800s. Further crossing created the Lleyn. Originally the ewes' milk was used for cheese-making.

The Lleyn is known for being an excellent and hardy mother, happy on lowland and on uplands up to 1,000 feet (305 meters) above sea level. In 1970, it was saved from extinction by a few breeders who formed the Lleyn Society. The breed is now safe and popular throughout the British Isles, Europe, the United States, New Zealand, and Australia. The wool is used for hand-knitting, hosiery, and dress fabrics; the coarser wool is used for carpets. The Lleyn also produces quality meat.

Lonk

Characteristics

The rams and ewes have curled horns.

Weight: ram 165–200 lb (75–91) kg, ewe 99–119 lb (45–54 kg)

Fleece weight: 4–7 lb (2.25–3 kg)

The Lonk has been bred on the Pennines in northern England from time immemorial; a flock in Lancashire can be traced back to 1740 when the sheep were farmed by the monks of Sawley and Whalley and on Rossendale Hill. It is said by many that the Lonk may be as old as the moors it grazes on. The Lonk is believed to have got its name from the northern word *lanky*, meaning a long, thin person. The breed is very hardy and can live throughout the year on the poorest of grazing on bleak, windswept moors 1,000–2,000 feet (305–610 meters) above sea level. This breed suffered severely during the foot-and-mouth epidemic of 2001.

Originally found only in East Lancashire, West Yorkshire, and North Derbyshire, it is now found throughout England. The fleece is white, and finest grades of Lonk wool are used for hand-knitting wool and blankets. The coarse wool is used for carpets, rugs, and tweed. The Lonk also produces top-quality meat.

Manx Loaghtan

Characteristics

The rams and ewes usually have four horns, but some have two, and some six. The horns on the rams are much stronger and heavier.

Weight: ram 121 lb (55 kg), ewe 88 lb (40 kg)

Fleece weight: 3 lb (1.5 kg)

The Manx Loaghtan, pronounced "locktun," are descendants of the primitive sheep found throughout Scotland and its islands. The newborn lambs are black, slowly turning brown, and over the next six to eight months will become the color of the adults. The breed has been grazing the hills of the Isle of Man for over 1,000 years and many believe it is a native of the island, while others believe that its origins are a prehistoric short-tailed breed found in isolated parts of northwestern Europe. From the eighteenth century, the numbers started to decline, and by the middle of the twentieth century there were fewer than fifty. Then the Manx National Heritage (a charitable trust) raised two healthy flocks, and this was the beginning of commercial flocks on the island. The future is definitely looking brighter, but there are still fewer than 1,500 breeding ewes in the British Isles.

The fleece is between fawn and a dark reddish brown, and craft spinners and weavers use the soft, richly colored, undyed wool to produce tweed and woolens. The meat is classed as a delicacy.

Montadale

Characteristics

Both rams and ewes are polled.

Weight: ram 200–275 lb (100–125 kg), ewe 160–180 lb (72–82 kg)

Fleece weight: 8–12 lb (3.5–5.5 kg)

The breed was developed in the 1930s, and much of the credit for that must go to E. H. Mattingly, a lamb buyer, who had for years dreamed of developing the ideal sheep. Its foundation lies in the Columbia and the Cheviot breeds, and over a period of nine years Mattingly achieved the desired standards for the Montadale, an amazing success. Many breeds have been developed in the United States, but the Montadale is the first to have been created by private enterprise.

This beautiful breed has an extremely white fleece, with very little lanolin (natural wool grease). Lanolin is good for the skin (my father used to bring some home from the textile mill where he worked—it worked wonders on my chilblains!). The fine-quality wool is used for knitting yarns and hosiery; the Montadale also produces quality meat.

Navajo-Churro

Characteristics

They can be horned or polled; the rams can have up to six horns.

Weight: ram 120–175 lb (55–79 kg), ewe 85–120 lb (38–55 kg)

Fleece weight: 4–6 lb (1.8–2.75 kg)

Usually called the Churro, this breed arrived in the Americas over 400 years ago courtesy of the Conquistadores and Don Juan Onate, and was the first domesticated breed to be introduced into what is now the United States. Today it is a rare breed. The Churro is a low-maintenance breed with a strong resistance to disease and is adaptable to extremes of temperature. The US government introduced a "Flock Reduction Scheme," and that initiative, coupled with crossbreeding, brought the breed to the point of extinction. In the 1970s, breeders began buying Churros and took on the task of preserving this beautiful breed.

The Churro has two coats: the soft undercoat provides insulation, while the coarse outer coat keeps the inner coat clean and repels rain and snow. The coat comes in a wide range of colors, reminiscent of the Shetland. The fleece color will frequently change as they mature; the black ones tending to go white with age. The indigenous Navajo tribe still uses the fleece to produce blankets and rugs. The meat is lean with a sweet, distinctive flavor.

North Country Cheviot

Characteristics

The rams can have horns and the ewes are polled.

Weight: ram 300 lb (136 kg), ewe 180 lb (82 kg)

Fleece weight: 8–10 lb (3.5–4.5 kg)

This is a strong-willed, independent, hardy breed, with a long, white fleece and a Roman nose with black nostrils. They have the ability to adapt and survive in most weather conditions. During the Highland Clearances in Scotland, the tenant farmers were removed, sometimes forcibly, to make way for this breed. The story begins in 1791 when Sir John Sinclair bought 500 ewes from farmers in the Cheviot Hills on the English–Scottish border; it is believed he crossed them with Border Leicester and the Leicester Longwool (known then as the English Leicester). The benefits of this cross ensured the sheep matured earlier and were larger, with longer wool.

They are excellent mothers, and the lambs will be feeding and running within minutes of being born. A shepherd once remarked that the North Country Cheviot is the only breed he had seen that would chase a dog out of the pasture and were the best-kept secret in the sheep industry. The wool is used in Scottish tweed and is favored by hand-spinners.

Oxford Down

Characteristics

The rams and ewes are without horns.

Weight: ram 243–309 lb (110–140 kg), ewe 201–249 lb (91–113 kg)

Fleece weight: 6–8 lb (2.5–3.5 kg)

The Oxford Down is the largest of the British Down breeds and originated in 1830 by crossing Cotswold rams with Hampshire Down and Southdown ewes. Between the mid-1950s and the 1970s, the breed became a victim of fashion, but a few breeders in the Midlands, Yorkshire, Northumberland, and the Scottish Borders kept the faith—and in the 1980s its popularity soared.

Originally it was found in the Cotswolds, South Wales, the Midlands, and parts of Yorkshire and Aberdeenshire, but now it is found throughout the UK and world on account of its meat and the ability to have lambs early in the year. This is a large sheep with a creamy white fleece and a "topknot." The lambs are well covered with wool and are not affected by the cold weather. The wool is used for hand-knitting yarns, Japanese futons, and blankets.

Romney

Characteristics

The rams and ewes are without horns but have a topknot.

Weight: ram 243 lb (110 kg),
ewe 187 lb (85 kg).
The American Romney is heavier.

Fleece weight: 7–11 lb (3–5 kg)

This breed has been seen on the Romney and North Kent marshes in southern England for 800 years. In the wool-smuggling days of the 1600s, the raising of sheep for the wool market was the most important element of trade on Romney Marsh. The Romney is probably the most numerous breed in the world. They are hardy and adaptable, and their feet are hard and strong; they have a resistance to foot rot and many other ailments that befall sheep living on damp ground. The Romney has a habit of spreading out evenly over the grazing area to make the best use of the pasture.

Found in the British Isles, originally in Kent and East Sussex, there are now flocks countrywide, as well as in the United States, Canada, New Zealand, and the Falkland Islands. The fleece is usually creamy white, and the wool is in great demand by hand-spinners and is also used for high-quality rugs, carpets, hosiery, hand-knitting wools, blankets, and carpets. Other natural fleece colors are black, gray, silver, and brown. The Romney produces top-quality meat.

Rouge de l'Ouest

Characteristics

The rams and ewes are polled.

Weight: ram 199–330 lb (90–150 kg), ewe 165–199 lb (75–90 kg)

Fleece weight: 3½–4¾ lb (1.5–2 kg)

The Rouge de l'Ouest ("Red of the West")—usually simplified to "the Rouge"—was developed in the Maine et Loire in west-central France, in the Pays de la Loire region, in the 1800s. It was created by crossing local Landrace sheep (adapted as a local traditional breed and in isolation) with the British Wensleydale and Bluefaced Leicester. The Rouge is now found throughout the British Isles and on most major continents. These are strong and powerful sheep, and with their short, dense, creamy white fleece are able to withstand the worst that Mother Nature throws their way.

Originally the Rouge was primarily a dairy breed, and its thick, rich milk was used to produce Camembert cheese. It is now bred as a dual-purpose breed, one of the main reasons it was imported into the British Isles. The meat is of excellent quality, and the short, fine wool is used for high-quality fabrics.

Ryeland

Characteristics

The rams and ewes are without horns.

Weight: ram 132 lb (60 kg), ewe 110 lb (50 kg)

Fleece weight: 4–7 lb (2–3 kg)

The breed originated in the Rye district of Herefordshire, England, over 800 years ago. It has been famous for 600 years, and is possibly the oldest recognized British sheep breed. In the thirteenth and fourteenth centuries, the wool was exported to Europe, mainly to Italy where it fetched the highest prices. It was known as "Lemster ore" (Lemster is the local name for Leominster) and had the same value as gold. By the sixteenth century, the breed's popularity had increased. Queen Elizabeth I was given a pair of Ryeland wool stockings and from then on would only wear clothing made from Ryeland wool.

This is a docile breed and easy to look after; given a supply of quality grass it will require no additional feed. The fleece is usually white, and the wool is used for high-quality tweed, hand-knitting wools, and hosiery. The other natural fleece colors are silver through to gray, black, brown, and fawn. It is found across the British Isles and most major continents. The Ryeland produces top-quality meat.

Shetland

Characteristics

The rams have beautifully rounded horns, and the ewes are without horns.

Weight: ram 90–150 lb (41–68 kg), ewe 75–100 lb (34–45 kg)

Fleece weight: 2–4 lb (0.9–2 kg)

The small Shetland sheep is believed to have been introduced to the Shetland Islands by the Vikings in the late eighth century and has developed in relative isolation ever since. The Shetland is small and tough, and easier to look after than many modern breeds. It can survive on poor land that is useless for any form of agriculture, but is also quite happy to live on better-quality grazing. The Islanders developed the breed to produce the finest wool of all indigenous British sheep. Shetland sheep can be any of the known sheep colors, although white and moorit (reddish brown) or black are the most common. There are eleven main colors and thirty different coat patterns, and more are being catalogued.

The wool is very popular with hand-spinners, and is also used for the famous Fair Isle sweaters, stockings, and tweed. This tough little British breed is now found countrywide as well as in Canada and the United States. The Shetland also produces high-quality meat.

Shropshire

Characteristics

The rams and ewes are without horns.

Weight: ram 225–290 lb (102–132 kg), ewe 170–200 lb (77–91 kg)

Fleece weight: 4–7 lb (2–3 kg)

Developed in the nineteenth century by improving the local Shropshire and Staffordshire breeds, these sheep are bred to survive on the Shropshire and Staffordshire hills in England. Shropshire sheep can adapt themselves to many types of pasture, including the very sparse, and can be found countrywide. Christmas tree growers in Scotland use the Shropshire to control ground weeds on their plantations.

These sheep have a greater covering of wool than similar breeds, the creamy white fleece being dense, heavy, and soft to handle. In the late nineteenth century, they were exported to the United States and Canada, and are also at home in Europe and Australia. The wool is used for hosiery, hand-knitting wools, and worsted suiting; large quantities are exported to Europe. The Shropshire is a source of top-quality meat.

Southdown

Characteristics

The rams can have horns.

Weight: ram 190–230 lb (86–104 kg), ewe 130–180 lb (59–81 kg)

Fleece weight: 5–8 lb (2.25–3.5 kg)

The Southdown is one of the oldest and most popular breeds and has been on the Sussex Downs since the 1700s. About 200 years ago, John Ellman realized its potential and started improving and standardizing the breed by selection from within his own flock, to achieve the breed as we know it today. The breed was then exported to New Zealand and was used for the foundation and development of the New Zealand "Canterbury Lamb." It was estimated that in 1341 there were 110,000 sheep in Sussex and in 1780 there was an estimated 200,000 sheep on the South Downs. Originally the breed was only found in the southeast of England, but it is now countrywide.

Docile and easy to handle, the Southdown with its dense white fleece and Roman nose was exported to the United States in the mid-nineteenth century, and can also be found happily grazing in New Zealand and Australia. Their excellent soft wool, one of the finest, is used in the manufacture of high-quality fabrics, hosiery, and hand-knitting wools. The Southdown also produces high-quality meat.

Suffolk

Characteristics

The rams and ewes are without horns.

Weight: ram 250–350 lb (110–160 kg), ewe 180–350 lb (80–160 kg)

Fleece weight 5–8 lb (2.25–3.6 kg)

The Suffolk is thought to have originated in Britain. Farmers crossing Southdown rams with Norfolk Horn ewes was first recorded in 1774 by the author Arthur Young, and the Suffolk was recognized as a pure breed in 1810. The breed is now found countrywide and across Europe as well as in Australia and New Zealand. It was exported to the United States in the late nineteenth century, and was the largest breed in the country at that time. It is now one of the most common purebred breeds in the United States.

The Suffolk is large and very muscular but has a gentle temperament. It is a distinctive and outstanding breed with its white fleece and black face and legs, and is said by many to be one of the most attractive of all sheep breeds. When the lambs are born they are various colors, but these disappear and change to white as they mature. The quality wool is used for hand-knitting yarns, tweed, and hosiery. The Suffolk also produces quality meat.

Swaledale

Characteristics

The rams and the ewes have curled horns, but the ram's horns are much larger.

Weight: ram 121–137 lb (55–62 kg), ewe 106–121 lb (48–55 kg)

Fleece weight: 3½–6 lb (1.5–2.5 kg)

The Swaledale is named after the valley of the River Swale in Yorkshire, and the sheep is the official symbol of the Yorkshire Dales. The breed was first registered in 1919, and there is very little earlier recorded history, but generations of farmers in North Yorkshire and Westmorland had specialized in breeding similar sheep. Found mainly on the Pennines in the northern counties of England, they are related to the Scottish Blackface and the Rough Fell.

The Swaledale sheep are very hardy and have a thick, creamy white fleece, just one of the reasons they are able to survive on the high and frequently wet moorlands. The fleece becomes grayer with age. The wool is used for tweed, rug wool, and the thicker hand-knitting yarns. The coarser wool is used for carpet manufacture. The Swaledale also produces top-quality meat.

Teeswater

Characteristics

The rams and ewes are without horns.

Weight: ram 250–300 lb (113–136 kg), ewe 150–250 lb (68–113 kg)

Fleece weight: 10–15 lb (4.5–6.75 kg)

The Teeswater is indigenous to Teesdale in County Durham in northern England and has been bred in the area for 200 years, first being mentioned in 1798. It is one of Britain's rarest breeds and is classed as "Vulnerable." It can now be found across the country and arrived in the United States in 1996; the Teeswater Sheep Society of North America has since worked hard supporting the breed and breeders, battling the government and red tape. The Teeswater has been crossbred with the Swaledale, Dalesbred, and Rough Fell, producing the well-known Masham.

The fleece is white to gray; the sheep are bred to have the characteristic chocolate brown or black markings on the nose, ears, and eyes. The long, curly locks hang individually, the length (staple) being 8–12 inches (20–30 centimeters). The wool is soft and supple and retains its curl and luster after washing and spinning; it is in great demand by hand-spinners and for worsted suiting, tweed, knitting wool, and carpets, and for blending with other fibers. It also produces top-quality meat.

Welsh Mountain Badger Face Torddu

Characteristics

The rams have dark spiral horns while the ewes are polled.

Weight: ram 111 lb–132 lb (50–60 kg), ewe 88–110 lb (40–50 kg)

Fleece weight: 3–5¾ lb (1.5–2.5 kg)

The Torddu ("torthee")—"black belly" in Welsh—is a very ancient breed of hardy mountain sheep with a white, gray, or light brown fleece and a distinct badger stripe over the eyes. There is also a black band running from the jaw to the belly and under the tail. It is difficult to define the breed's origin with any certainty, but it was mentioned in the seventh century and later in the *Domesday Book* (1086). The breed became less popular in the Middle Ages when there was a greater demand by the wool traders for white wool. They were first described as "badger face" in the 1600s.

They are usually seen in Wales, but small flocks are found throughout the country. Torddu ewes are excellent mothers. Today the majority of wool is used for carpets. Torddu are primarily a meat breed, producing delectable lamb from any grazing.

Welsh Mountain Badger Face Torwen

Characteristics

Rams have dark spiral horns, while the ewes are polled.

Weight: ram 110–132 lb (50–60 kg), ewe 88–110 lb (40–50 kg)

Fleece weight: 3–5¾ lb (1.5–2.5 kg)

The Torwen (Welsh for "white belly") is a very ancient breed of hardy mountain sheep that was mentioned in the *Domesday Book*. They are less numerous than the Torddu sheep. The fleece is black, but fades to brown in the sunlight and there is a distinct white badger stripe above the eyes, a slightly smaller stripe than that on the Torddu. The breed is found mainly in Wales, but small flocks are found around the UK.

The breed has, for the past ten years, had the greatest number of entries in the Royal Welsh Show, averaging 200 (more than any other native breed). The Torwen are excellent mothers, and they produce quality meat from any grazing. The majority of the wool is used for carpets, but it is also in great demand by hand-spinners who prefer to use the undyed wool.

Wensleydale

Characteristics

Rams and ewes are without horns.

Weight: ram 300 lb (136 kg), ewe 250 lb (114 kg).

Fleece weight: 13½–20 lb (6–9 kg).

The Wensleydale, found throughout the British Isles, in Europe, and in the United States, is a longwool breed of sheep. It was developed in a small hamlet near Bedale in North Yorkshire, England, using a ram called Bluecap, which was born in 1839.

Bluecap's parents were a Dishley ram and a longwool ewe of a type that is now extinct. The crossbred sheep the Masham was sired first by Wensleydale rams and later by Teeswater rams. The Wensleydale has a long, curly, white fleece and a long, curly topknot that is never sheared, purely because it would detract from the beauty of the animal. The soft Wensleydale wool is the finest luster wool in the world and is in great demand by hand-spinners, and is used for high-quality knitting and weaving yarns. The wool hangs down in curly ringlets up to 6 inches (15 centimeters) long. The Wensleydale is also a source of top-quality meat.

ACKNOWLEDGEMENTS

I must thank owners, breeders, breed societies and associations, and enthusiasts for their help. Without their unflagging enthusiasm and willingness to answer a stream of questions, I would sit in front of a blank monitor. Thank you to all my family members, whose pithy comments spur me on to readable text. Any mistakes are mine and mine alone.

Many thanks to my wife, Elaine, my daughters, Ruth and Karen, and my granddaughter, Rebecca, for all their help.

I would like to acknowledge the help and advice received from the following people: Ólafur R. Dýrmundsson PhD, National Adviser on Organic Farming and Land Use, Iceland; and Tony Harman of Maple Leaf Images, Skipton, North Yorkshire, for photographic help and advice. Thanks go to Bonnie J. Barcus of Spin Dance Acres in Boise, Idaho, for being my US eyes and ears.

PICTURE CREDITS

(**Animal icons**) DOLININAN/Shutterstock; (**front cover, top**) Galileo30/Shutterstock; (**front cover, bottom L to R**) Heath Johnson/Shutterstock, Big Joe/Shutterstock, Svetlana Foote/Shutterstock, Budimir Jevtic/Shutterstock; (**back cover and page 1, L to R**) Nick Beer/Shutterstock, Jeremy-Stenuit/Shutterstock, Zulkifli Ishak, kvasilev/Shutterstock, Victoria Everleigh (*www.westilkerton.co.uk*); (**pages 2–3**) Sara Winter/Shutterstock; (**page 5**) White Park Cattle Society; (**page 6**) Beck Polder Photography/Shutterstock; (**page 7**) Ariene Studio/Shutterstock; (**page 44**) Michael Conrad/Shutterstock; (**page 45**) MarcvanKessel.com/Shutterstock; (**page 84**) Pierluigi. Palazzi/Shutterstock; (**page 85**) Artsiom Petrushenka/Shutterstock; (**page 114**) Cerovsek Barbara/Shutterstock; (**page 115**) Martin Prochazkacz/Shutterstock; (**page 142**) JuliusKielaitis/Shutterstock; (**page 143**) Brian Cox; (**page 188**) Jon Beard/Shutterstock

Chickens

Page (8) Pear Tree Poultry; (9) David Brandreth; (10) Linnea Hendrickson; (11) David Brandreth; (12) Jim Dale; (13) David Brandreth; (14) David Brandreth; (15) W. and K. Pimlott; (16) David Brandreth; (17) David Brandreth; (18) Chalk Hill Poultry; (19) David Brandreth; (20) Kath Austen; (21) David Brandreth; (22) Big W Ranch; (23) Big W Ranch; (24) John and Sylvia Cook; (25) David Brandreth; (26) Robert and Veronica Potter; (27) Julie Connell; (28) David Brandreth; (29) David Brandreth; (30) Brockscombe Valley Farm; (31) David Brandreth; (32) David Brandreth; (33) David Brandreth; (34) Mikaela Rodriguiz; (35) David Brandreth; (36) David Brandreth; (37) Brockscombe Valley Farm; (38) Chalk Hill Poultry; (39) Rolf Piepenbring; (40) David Brandreth; (41) Wanda Zwart; (42) David Brandreth; (43) David Brandreth.

Cows

Page (46) Wedderlie Aberdeen Angus; (47) Ayrshire Cattle Society; (48) The Belted Galloway Cattle Society; (49) Welsh Black Cattle Society; (50) British Bazadaise Cattle Society; (51) British Blonde Cattle Society; (52) British Blue Cattle Society: photograph by kind permission of Norbreck Genetics; (53) British White Cattle Society; (54) Cimarron Brown Swiss; (55) The British Charolais Cattle Society Ltd; (56) The Devon Cattle Breeders Society; (57) The Dexter Cattle Society; (58) Holstein UK; (59) Helen McCann; (60) The British Gelbvieh Cattle Society; (61) English Guernsey Cattle Society; (62) Hereford Cattle Society; (63) Sheila Foster-Hancock; (64) Holstein UK; (65) Irish Moiled Cattle Society: photograph courtesy of Michelle McCauley; (66) National Milk Records; (67) Esther Moliné; (68) British Limousin Cattle Society; (69) Lincoln Red Cattle Society; (70) The Longhorn Cattle Society; (71) Paul Basnett; (72) Ben Beddoes – Dairy Dreams; (73) Gillian Harries; (74) The British Parthenaise Cattle Society; (75) Marc Venema/Shutterstock; (76) Red Poll Cattle Society; (77) Bob Gibbons/Alamy; (78) James Robinson; (79) Claude@Munich; (80) South Devon Herd Book Society; (81) Timothy Hart; (82) Highland Wagyu: photograph courtesy of Catherine MacGregor Photography; (83) White Park Cattle Society; photograph courtesy of Lawrence Alderson.

Goats

Page (86) Margot Wolfs; (87) Ian Preston; (88) Michael Trotter; (89) The Bagot Goat Society; (90) Mariagrazia Arrighini; (91) Zulkifli Ishak; (92) Paul Mounter; (93) Clive Dodd; (94) Martin Kaufmann; (95) Candi Morgan McCorkle, Rustling Oaks Farm; (96) Steve Bates; (97) Johanna B. Thorvaldsdottir, Haafell Geitfjarsetur; (98) Hancock Kiko Farm; (99) Kelsee Gibbs at Kinder Korner Goats; (100) Lance Hays; (101) Courtesy of ANGBA ˝ Bessie Miller; (102) Erin Hottle; (103) Gillian Cunningham, Willow Tree Farm; (104) Levend Landgoed NOVA; (105) Hilary Breakell, Marshview Viggo; (106) Little Bit Acres; (107) Brian Goodwin; (108) Jeannette Beranger; (109) ˝ Lindy Warner Photography; (110) Morgan Fredericks; (111) Miche`le Hennin; (112) Willowbank Toggenburgs; (113) Paul Asman and Jill Lenoble.

Pigs

Page (116) Jim Perkins; (117) Berkshire Pig Breeders Club; (118) Miquel Nieto, ibergour.co.uk; (119) Oaklands Pigs; (120) Trevaskis Farm/ Bob Berry Photography; (121) Oaklands Pigs; (122) Professor D. Phillip Sponenberg, DVM, PhD, ACT (Honorary); (123) Jan Walton; (124) Oaklands Pigs; (125) John and Zeller Penner; (126) ML Farms, Mason, Texas; (127) Courtesy ACMC Ltd; (128) Piggywiggy's (Michael & Therese Duffey); (129) Oaklands Pigs; (130) Teresa Watson, Agriculture and Horticulture Development Board; (131) Pig Paradise Farm, Tony York; (132) Courtesy ACMC Ltd; (133) Courtesy ACMC Ltd; (134) Emile DeFelice; (135) Yorkshire Meats; (136) Gillo Fawr Pedigree Pietrain; (137) Esther Gallant; (138) Oaklands Pigs; (139) Helen and Rob Rose; (140) Turner & Sons Landhill Herd; (141) The New England Boar Company.

Sheep

Page (144) Elle Gator; (145) Ross F. Mitchell; (146) Andy Stables; (147) Ambersky235; (148) Robert Whitcombe; (149) Mike Eckley; (150) Pam James; (151) Ambersky235; (152) John Ward; (153) Alison Green, Devon Closewool Sheep Breeders Society; (154) David Brennan; (155) Barry Marsh; (156) Griffiths Mill; (157) Victoria Eveleigh, *www.westilkerton.co.uk*; (158) Lily Warne Wool; (159) Brian Cox; (160) © Wendy McDonnell, *www.wendsphotography.co.uk*; (161) Tracey Evans; (162) Matt Ertle; (163) Ambersky235; (164) Katahdin Hair Sheep International, Inc., *www.katahdins.org*; (165) Margaret Collins; (166) S. and A. Glover – Windy Ridge Flock; (167) Lincoln Longwool Sheep Breeders Association; (168) Lawrence Wright; (169) Lleyn Sheep Society; (170) Lonk Sheep Breeders Association; (171) Katie Fuller, katiefuller.co.uk; (172) Kendra Fleck, Montadale Sheep Breeders Association; (173) Bonnie J. Barcus, Spin Dance Acres, Boise, ID; (174) Ambersky235; (175) Oxford Down Sheep Breeders Association; (176) *www.adamswainephotography@gmail.com*; (177) Agnès Legrand; (178) Moira Linaker; (179) Pete Glanville, Shetland Organics; (180) Shropshire Sheep Breed Association; (181) Nicki G. Kent; (182) Jack Geerts, Watford, Ontario; (183) Ambersky235; (184) Teeswater Breeders Association Ltd; (185) Douglas Law; (186) Veronika Hubris; (187) WLSBA/E. L. Sherwin.

INDEX